THE
Career Clinic

THE
Career Clinic —

EIGHT SIMPLE RULES FOR FINDING WORK YOU LOVE

Maureen Anderson

AMACOM

AMERICAN MANAGEMENT ASSOCIATION

NEW YORK ■ ATLANTA ■ BRUSSELS ■ CHICAGO ■ MEXICO CITY ■ SAN FRANCISCO ■
SHANGHAI ■ TOKYO ■ TORONTO ■ WASHINGTON, D.C.

Special discounts on bulk quantities of AMACOM books are available to corporations, professional associations, and other organizations. For details, contact Special Sales Department, AMACOM, a division of American Management Association, 1601 Broadway, New York, NY 10019.
Tel: 212-903-8316. Fax: 212-903-8083.
E-mail: specialsls@amanet.org
Website: www.amacombooks.org/go/specialsales
To view all AMACOM titles go to: www.amacombooks.org

This publication is designed to provide accurate and authoritative information in regard to the subject matter covered. It is sold with the understanding that the publisher is not engaged in rendering legal, accounting, or other professional service. If legal advice or other expert assistance is required, the services of a competent professional person should be sought.

Library of Congress Cataloging-in-Publication Data

Anderson, Maureen, 1958–
   The career clinic : eight simple rules for finding work you love / Maureen Anderson.
      p. cm.
   Includes index.
   ISBN-13: 978-0-8144-1051-6 (pbk.)
   ISBN-10: 0-8144-1051-0 (pbk.)
   1. Vocational interests. 2. Job satisfaction. 3. Conduct of life. I. Title.

HF5381.5.A53 2009
650.14—dc22

2008028767

Printing number
10 9 8 7 6 5 4 3 2 1

to the memory of Ben Pritchard

CONTENTS

PREFACE

I am afraid to die.

I know this because for a while, I wasn't. I was writing my first book, and so immersed in work I loved that it was as if magic dust had been sprinkled on everything. I was filled with such a sense of purpose and peace that if someone had asked me what I thought about dying, I think I would have brushed off the question. "Well, whatever," I can imagine having said. "I just want to get back to my book."

The minute I turned in the manuscript, it returned—what Gregg Levoy, author of *Callings*, calls a low-grade, background anxiety about death.

It made me think the secret to life is doing the work we are meant to do.

It was also about this time I began hosting a radio program that helps people find work they love. Since then I've done hundreds of interviews and met many people who not only love their work, but live without regret. They don't necessarily define themselves by their work, but it was their foundation—the starting place from which their lives evolved. As someone put it, they know where they're going, whom they want to take along, and what they want the scenery to be like.

I want to share some of their stories with you because I believe they have something important to teach us about how to live.

Levoy thinks we want to die "with a yes on our lips and not a no. We don't want to enter kingdom come kicking and screaming and begging for more time."

I don't want to, anyway. I don't want to get to the end of the road and find out my life hasn't added up to anything. I want to run a subtotal now, so I can make adjustments.

Most of all I want to be like the monk in Bernie Siegel's *Prescriptions for Living*. When asked what he would do if he had only fifteen minutes left to live, he smiled, said "This"—and went back to his gardening.

ONE

No Regrets

They never warn you. The old ones. There should be volumes written on it. There should be billboards proclaiming it on every street corner. Government pamphlets should be printed up and distributed to every citizen. But as it is, only the old ones know, and they never tell. They keep it to themselves like one final inside joke. Passing knowing glances and head nods. This is for them to know and for the rest of us to find out. And we, all of us, do find out eventually—when it's too late to do anything about it.

We grow up hearing the worn adages: Time flies, time is of the essence, there's no time like the present. Words of wisdom that we commit to memory and never completely grasp. We never took it seriously, not really. We should have been shaken awake, slapped hard across the face, somehow been made to appreciate fully the preciousness of time.

—Greg Crosby, *Newsweek*

I've already mentioned that I'm afraid to die. Since writing that, I've made peace with the concept—to some extent. But my peace was tested recently. A routine medical test came back with the recommendation to get more tests. For twenty hours or so, I was in a place I'd never been before, and it wasn't fear I felt, only grief.

If more tests confirmed there was something to worry about, what would I do then? How could I say good-bye to my sweethearts? I wasn't afraid to die. I just didn't want to.

There wasn't room for much of anything else. Just sadness at the thought of saying good-bye.

Work did cross my mind, though. What, exactly, have I contributed? Has it mattered that I've been here? And in those scary moments, it wasn't the past I was thinking about. It was now. What am I up to *now*? I thought of two things: this book, and a speech I was giving a few weeks later that terrified me.

They were comfort, those two things, because I was still reaching—and that's all that mattered. Giving myself a chance to matter. Not knowing how my story's going to turn out, but not minding—because I'm still having fun writing it, still excited to turn the page.

Before this health scare I would have told you I was on speaking terms with death. What a crock. I had no idea. But I can report there isn't much I've changed, having had a glimpse of just how much I love my life. From now on

I want to do more of what I've been doing, become more me, throw myself out there with more abandon.

When I interview people for *The Career Clinic* we often talk about death. We begin with the end, as the saying goes. How do you want it to have mattered that you were here? Now do *that.*

Gregg Levoy

CALLINGS

Consult your death.

Given the fact, the brute, existential fact that you're going to die and be a million years dead, what do you want to do with this little nick of time? What do you really want to do?

I agree with Nietzsche, who said that life is a thousand times too short to bore ourselves. And I wonder if your life flashed before your eyes, would it hold your interest?

Some people consider me an expert on finding work you love because of a book I wrote, *Callings*. I first started working on the book in 1993, though I didn't realize it at the time. I was living in Taos, New Mexico, and teaching a workshop for writers called "The True Material." Essentially it was a four-day retreat, and it was about how to know that you're writing what you really need to be writing. I had started to teach the workshops with my partner, Robin, and one day I was sitting at my computer preparing for another one. I had an inch-thick stack of notes sitting there, and she walked in and looked at it. "It looks like you're writing a book rather than preparing for a workshop," she said. And I realized either I was grossly overpreparing or she was right.

I tried writing the book for writers for about six months, and kept hitting a brick wall. Then one afternoon I had a revelation. The book wanted to get bigger; I wanted to help everyone find his true material.

I had a sense while I was writing *Callings* of absolute rightness. A question I get asked a lot is, "How do you figure out whether this is a true calling that comes from a deeper, higher place, or just the ego, wishful thinking, or even a desire for escape?" So I was looking at this sense of rightness that I had, and that was one of the clear signals—that this was definitely the book that wanted to be written through me. It was an absolute feeling of being on the ball, being in line with what really wanted to come through me, and a sense that it was also aligned with my deeper values. The book just felt absolutely right all the way along.

At the moment, my calling is to take the book out on the road. Being on the road is healing and satisfies the other side of my personality. It's the antidote to the isolation of writing. That's what I've been doing ever since the book came out, workshops and lectures, to the point where, when people ask me what I do, my old standby, "I'm a writer," doesn't even feel quite right anymore. Now I would say, first and foremost, I'm a teacher.

People ask me what a calling is. Before I answer, I like to point out that it's easy to scare the daylights out of yourself by thinking a calling has to be something exalted, like the ministry. It doesn't. It doesn't have to relate to work at all. An intuition is a calling, a dream is a calling, a body symptom is a calling. Literally, the word *symptom* means sign, so it is therefore also a calling. Intuition, dreams, and symptoms are like fire drills for the bigger calls. I think paying attention to the smaller ones can help you recognize the big ones when they appear.

All the religions of the world seem to agree that dreams are one of the channels through which the gods traditionally speak to mortals. I think by paying attention to your dreams, promising yourself that you will interpret them as best you can and attend to them, and just in general honoring them, you will bring all sorts of incredible insights and instructions into your life. Why sleep through them?

That said, I have had to cultivate patience on the order of years for callings to come through. The kind of passion and clarity I felt while writing *Callings*, that this is what I was put on the earth to do, has seemed to come in waves. In between, I'm just hanging there, awaiting further instructions, my marching orders. The key for me is to keep asking the question. However long it takes, I keep asking for dreams, keep paying attention to my intuition, keep looking at my loves and my hates. I pay attention to all those little emotional tropisms: what I move toward, what I move away from. Eventually there's a significant clustering of signals that indicates, okay, this is what's next.

When I was writing the book I had this overwhelming anxiety that I wouldn't live long enough to finish it. I've never had this feeling before, but I was afraid I would get into an accident or something would happen to prevent me from fulfilling what felt like a piece of destiny to me. I was so immensely relieved when it was over. It felt like, now's a good time to die. I could die fulfilled because at least I made this contribution to the world and got this proverbial music out of me.

I have since come back to my usual, low-grade, background anxiety about death, which of course just means there's still more inside of me I want to get out.

At any given time I want to feel like I'm really using myself up, that I'm using the gifts that I have, not just giving a generous tip of the hat to them, but really making the most of them.

David Sutherland

FILMMAKER

I am a documentary portraitist.

I make my living producing films that are totally driven by the audio. You can hear and feel the characters from as much as a hundred yards away, like you're living in their skin, and that's really what drives the plot—the feeling that you're so close to these people you're a part of the family. I joke that I do the PBS version of reality TV. It's not cost-effective. There can be more than a half million pieces of audio in a single film that you have to painstakingly edit, and on one film it took me nineteen weeks just to do that.

The production I'm most known for is *The Farmer's Wife.* The goal with my work is to portray the cost and value of a dream. In this film I wanted to put a face on the people who were chasing the dream of family farming. I was looking for a woman who had something in her voice. I had never even met Juanita Buschkoetter when I decided she was the one. I talked to her on the phone and just knew. She had a catch in her voice, and she spoke from her heart.

I fell in love with Nebraska while we were doing this film. You can be on the street and hear people talking a quarter mile away. Depending on which way the wind is blowing, you can hear exactly what they're saying. That's part of what gave me the inspiration to use several microphones while we were taping. I used as many as six at once. They're wireless, they're in their shirts, and Juanita and her husband got so used to them being there it's like they weren't. I'd be in a kitchen cupboard monitoring sound and Juanita would be putting dishes away and she'd slam the cupboard doors into me like I was part of the furniture, she was that into what she was talking about.

We were with Juanita and her husband when they woke up, and we stayed with them until they went to bed. Then we went back to the motel room for some editing, before getting up at six the next morning and starting all over again. It took years to make this film, and there were many times I could identify with the Buschkoetters more than I would have liked. We went through two-thirds of our retirement money on the production, and in some ways it was the lowest point of my life. You don't even want to know how many people told me I was out of my mind, doing what I was doing. There were no programmers who, before they saw footage from *The Farmer's Wife*, said anyone would watch six and a half hours about a farm family.

And you know what? The show had 18 million viewers. It came out the day the videotape of Bill Clinton's grand jury testimony in the Monica Lewinsky sex scandal was released. It also coincided with the season premier of *Monday Night Football* and the debut of the new sitcoms in the fall schedule. By the third night, the website had more than 800,000 hits and we had received more than 30,000 e-mails. It's the only prime-time PBS broadcast where the ratings were almost three times higher on the third night than they were on the first night. Not even *The Civil War* was as popular.

So, why did people watch? Because they can relate to a dream. No matter how improbable the dream may be, there's a hunger for stories of how people go after it anyway.

I was the proverbial medium as message.

And all this acclaim, all this satisfaction of knowing I have done something that really mattered, would not have happened had my tire store not been hit by lightning. Yeah. That's what I was doing before I got into filmmaking. I was selling tires.

I had done one film, about an old man, which was shot in a railroad car diner. I didn't have any money then, and it wasn't beautifully shot. But one of my relatives was seeing a woman who said her brother-in-law would like that film. Turns out he was a cameraman for *National Geographic.* He saw my style, liked it, and helped me get my next film produced—about a painter. That one made it to the Berlin Film Festival and was well received.

But I had a family and couldn't ask them to support me while I went off and did something as indulgent as make films. So I sold tires. I never forgot my dream, but something was holding me back.

That stroke of lightning was almost like the earth opening up. We were underinsured. My safety net was gone, as were my excuses. There was nothing left to do but go after the dream.

So my question to you is this: Are you selling tires because you've always wanted to sell tires? I know some people do—I met a few while I was making *The Farmer's Wife*. But if you're selling tires because you're afraid to make films, I have another question. Is that what you want your kids to learn about life—that you give up on your dreams? Maybe more importantly, what kind of a gift is that for your future self—the one the doctor turns to someday and says the cancer is inoperable? They say it's never too late to go after a dream, but they are wrong.

Here's wishing you the courage to go after your dreams, or a stroke of lightning. Or both.

Valerie Young

DREAMER IN RESIDENCE

As cubicle jobs go, mine was pretty good. Well, except for the ninety-minute commute. But it was a Fortune 500 company, management job, good money.

Then my mother died.

She was sixty-one.

She was five months from retiring.

It was one of those moments when you ask yourself, *What am I doing?*

Three months later, I quit my job. I took another one closer to home, nothing I was crazy about, but it freed up the time I used to spend commuting to plot my escape from corporate life. I eventually founded ChangingCourse .com, a community of people who aspire to what I've discovered—that you don't need a job to earn a living.

As you can read on my website, I feel blessed with riches no amount of money can buy. I have a comfortable, two-minute commute from my bedroom to my home office. I can take off in the middle of the day for a walk—and when it's warm enough, to enjoy my garden.

I've heard from thousands of people around the world who are determined to change their course.

There are some very creative and interesting ways people are doing that these days. One of my favorite course changers is a man who never forgot how much he loved building sandcastles when he was a kid. Now his company has that love as its foundation. He builds elaborate sand sculptures and gets commissions from all over the world.

Another favorite story is about the new mom who enlisted my help after her first child was born. I'd suggested she get out her calendar and set a date for being in business for herself. "It scared me to death," she told me later. "But I did it anyway. And it made all the difference. It made my dream real." She called me to say she was starting a marketing and events planning company and was thrilled.

My advice is always the same. Think about how you want your life to look, then build the livelihood around that life.

Richard Goldman

MYSTERY LOVER

My wife and I had been working normal jobs when she had a severe asthma attack that put her in the hospital. She was the executive director of the Allegheny County Center for Victims of Violent Crimes, and I was in the software business. Both of us had been feeling stressed, burned out. When Mary Alice went into the hospital we started to think about the direction our lives were taking and talk about what we'd rather be doing.

The rule in the software business is: "The customer is never happy." There's always something else they want the program to do. My entire life was listening to, "Why doesn't it do this? Why does it do it this way? Why can't it do it that way?" There were ranges of unhappy. Good was when they were sort of close to neutral, and then it just got worse from there.

So when Mary Alice got sick, we had all the inspiration we needed to change our lives. We were in our forties. We'd been making good money, but we hadn't been spending all of it. We'd been reasonably frugal, hadn't created a lifestyle that wedded us to huge salaries. And so we thought about what to do that would be more fun than what we had been doing.

We'd always liked bookstores and often talked about owning one, but we realized that this idea of "someday, when we're retired, we'll open a bookstore someplace" was ridiculous. No one, at that stage in his or her life, would be prepared to do what you have to do to start a business. If we were going to do it, it would have to be now—while we were capable of achieving our dream. That's when we opened the Mystery Lovers Bookshop.

Everything was a challenge. How big would the inventory be? How many feet of shelves would we need for that much inventory? We had to open accounts with publishers, which isn't easy as a new business owner because you don't have much of anything to tell them. We had to figure everything out. We knew so little about retail business that our cash drawer is backward—one-dollar bills on the left, contrary to the universal practice in retail.

It was hard work, and it continues to be. But with the possible exception of filling out tax forms, it's all important and necessary work. By that I mean, when I'm unpacking books and shelving them, I'm not standing around wondering what idiot decided I should do that. It just has to be done. It's not like completing the quarterly sales forecast.

Mary Alice and I can sit down over dinner and decide that it would be great if we did such and such a promotion.

And the next morning we do it. There's no committee. There are no memos. We just decide what to do, and do it. It's a very pure way to live.

The bookstore's been so successful that I'm often asked why we don't franchise it. And I say, "Why? So I would end up sitting at a desk talking on the phone all day, like I used to do?" No thanks.

You want to live without regret? Start in your twenties. The way you choose to live in young adulthood determines what you're able to do in the second part of your life. If you trade up the new house every two years, lease the big cars, insist on a membership to the exclusive clubs, whatever it is, you've given yourself a death sentence. If you're completely in debt, spending every dime you get your hand on, know this: You're going to be a slave to that lifestyle until you drop dead from a massive coronary.

My advice is, don't do that to yourself. Save your money. You'll be saving your life.

Jay Gubrud

MOTIVATIONAL SPEAKER

Spring 1992. I get a call on a Saturday morning. It's my dad and he's crying. Mom was gone. She'd been battling cancer for more than a year, and she had died the night before. I don't remember much about the next few months. They were a blur. Then three months after my mom's death, and I mean to the day, my grandfather—her dad—died. I had recently graduated from college and was having trouble finding the energy to look for a job. When Grandpa died he took the rest of that energy with him. But I found a sales job and thought, well, I'll do the best I can to get on with my life. And one month after that, my best friend killed himself with a shotgun.

The thing that probably saved me was the sales training I was going through at the time. They send you to see these speakers who can supposedly help you become a better salesperson. Have you ever been to a sales seminar? Even if you're not the outgoing type, you're bound to be fired up by the time the evening is over. Which was exactly what I needed back then. I needed inspiration to go on living. And it was fascinating, how taken the audience was with the speaker. In one life-changing moment I said to myself, "I want to do *that.*"

I knew I probably had enough stories to share just from what I had been through those past six months, so I started pitching my services as a motivational speaker. I spoke at low-risk venues to begin with: service clubs, church groups, whoever would have me. The first time I got up in front of a group I crashed and burned. It was so bad it seemed like I spent the next week in tears. But I got up the nerve to try it again, and I choked again. And I felt terrible for about three hours. This was progress. So I went out and gave another speech. I sucked that time too, but I only felt bad for about ten minutes. Because even though I'd sucked, I hadn't sucked as much. I was getting better. I was getting better, I was having fun, and I had a dream.

Now I speak to audiences of 1,200 people on up. I am so thankful for training in sales because when you're in business for yourself, you're looking for work every day of your life. I'm doing much more selling than I ever did as a "salesperson." But I'm also doing much more good in the world. At least it feels that way.

I get e-mail from people who remember me from a speech I gave years ago. A recent one was from a woman who said I'm still "in her world," inspiring her. I had a big impact on her life and I improved it, which is what I live for.

You've probably heard all the clichés—when people talk about their biggest fears, public speaking ranks right up there with death. But life's a roller coaster. If you're not scared out of your mind, it's not fun. It's boring. Let's say you already know every twist and turn and are *sure* you'll survive it. Where's the adventure in that?

I'm the guy in the seat behind you on the roller coaster. I'm the one screaming, "We're all going to die! We're all going to die!"

Oh, and the maniac who tramples you in his rush to get back in line for another ride? That's me, too.

Mary Jane Ballou

HARPIST

I used to be a librarian in New York City. I worked my way up to library director, and like to say that I was very successful at leading someone else's life. As any good librarian, I approached problems with research. When it was time to design a new life, that's the form my scheming took. I started at one end of the self-help, career-change section and worked my way to the other . . . but I never did anything. When I got particularly restless, I'd just read another book.

Then I had a stroke. The doctor in the emergency room smiled at me when he said, "I really think you should consider some lifestyle changes."

And that was it. It was as if I needed permission to put all the books down and go live. I put my very nice apartment on the market and told everyone I was going to "find myself"—hopefully in Florida. The people I thought would be the most horrified were actually the most supportive, and I wondered how often that plays out. We never come right out and ask parents or spouses or children what they think of this plan or that—we just guess which things they would disapprove of and chart our course accordingly. But all they really want, usually, is for us to be happy. What a shame to not know that, to not even ask.

I'm trained as a musician, but I had put that aside for the practical and sensible library world. Every now and then, I noticed that the people who weren't quite so practical and sensible seemed to be having more fun than I was. Then I'd read another book until the feeling passed.

Everything changed when I realized I, too, was going to die. I returned to music and built up a business. I play the harp at weddings, funerals, and everything in between. It wasn't easy, getting established. I was scared probably three times a day and once during the night. It is very scary to overhaul your life, and anyone who tells you it isn't is a liar. When I got frightened I made a list of things I could do to advance my dream. The list was filled with tiny things—make one phone call, send two e-mails, whatever. But I didn't freeze up.

If I was so hysterical I couldn't even make a list, I cleaned the bathroom. It's hard to worry really successfully when you're cleaning the bathroom. After it was sparkling, I was probably not one bit closer to my dream. But at least I had a clean bathroom.

You don't even want to know how often—and it's been years—I tell myself that if this new life doesn't work out I can go back to being a librarian. But I make myself wait one more day, and then one more day after that. It's beginning to pay off. I'm living without regret, one day at a time.

TWO

Talk to Yourself

Being able to reflect on your life while you're living it (instead of in the instant before you die) is one key to fulfillment, however you go about it. When you're working full-time, though, quiet time can seem like just one more thing to do in an already overcrowded schedule.

—Joe Dominguez and Vicki Robin,
Your Money or Your Life

Once upon a time, I wished I could take a class on how to make a life transition. I'd never heard of anything like that, but I needed it desperately. I saw a mention of an upcoming meeting for women in communications. I showed up, got my little name tag, and took a seat. I was so distracted by the upheaval in my life, I couldn't focus on what the speaker was saying. Toward the end of her talk, the woman said, "If you do nothing else for yourself, pick up a copy of this book." It was *What Color Is Your Parachute?* "Get the book," she said, "and read it. If you don't read it, at the very least, go through the appendices. I promise it will be the best thing you ever do for your career."

I had read *Parachute* in high school. "I know all that," I remember thinking. Then I chose civil engineering as my major in college. Nothing could have been less suited to my personality. Now I wondered if I should read the book again, more thoroughly.

I bought the latest edition of *Parachute*, started thumbing through the appendices, and came upon a photograph of a resort and the words, "Fifteen days of life/work planning. . . ." Before I read any further, I knew I had to get there: The Inn of the Seventh Mountain in Bend, Oregon. Dick Bolles, author of *Parachute*, was the leader of the workshop. I signed up, and I'll tell you what happened a little later. For now it's worth mentioning that when I set out for Bend I could have sworn I had no idea what I wanted to do with my life. When I left two weeks later, armed with a plan to embark on a radio and writing career, I realized I had always known.

Career consultant Michael Bryant puts it this way. "I have yet to see a person have the following reaction to figuring out what they want to do: 'I never knew I liked that.' Of course you know."

So why did it take me so long to discover this? Maybe because I didn't believe having a good time was the point, even, or perhaps especially, in our careers. The old, "Why do you think they call it work?" Then Dick Bolles, who literally wrote the book on life transitions, came along and turned my model upside down. He presented what was to me a new way of looking at not just work, but life—and it sounded fun. The way I had been going about it hadn't worked. There was nothing to lose.

I quit thinking in terms of whether my plans made sense to other people. It wasn't their lives we were talking about.

Michael Bryant

PARTY OF ONE

I was an athlete in high school and college, so coaching sports—and teaching school—was the track I'd laid out for myself. Which was fine for a couple of years. Then one morning it hit me faster than you read the last sentence. I was in front of a group of ninth-graders, talking about the Missouri Compromise at eight o'clock in the morning, and a little voice inside said, "I don't know what I'm going to be doing when I'm forty, but it's not going to be this."

I thought back to what excited me when I was the age my students were. Even as a kid I loved running businesses. I had five by the time I was eleven—raking leaves, shoveling snow, things like that. So I decided I'm one of those people who wants to do what he wants to do, when he wants to do it, the way he wants to do it. Once you know that about yourself, you can't unknow it. That's when I struck out on my own. It wasn't easy. My first business—helping kids decide what they want to do after high school—failed, but now I have a thriving one, helping people live effectively. And I've learned a few things.

Like this: We keep our dreams distant as a way of not messing them up.

People tell me, "I don't know what I want out of life." I respond with, "Oh yes you do." And you wouldn't believe how many times they immediately say, "Oh. Okay. I'll tell you." I might have to reassure them the door's closed and I won't tell anybody. But they know. You know.

My theory is that it's scary to cop to dreams. We think if we keep them where they are, safely tucked away in our mind, and never attempt them, then we can't fail. But we are wrong. When you die, it won't be the failures you regret. It will be the things you wanted that you didn't go after.

What's the worst thing that will happen if you go after a dream? You'll fail? So you fail. Like that doesn't happen all the time anyway. So you fail at something that counts. There's a concept.

How old were you when you decided failure was a bad thing? When we're very young, we're taught that accomplishment includes making mistakes and that failure is just a natural part of the process. When a one-year-old is learning to walk and falls down, we say, "That's okay. That's okay. Keep going." And the one-year-old, to my knowledge, is not thinking, "I can't do it. I'll never be able to do it. I'll still be crawling when I'm twenty. The kid next door, he was walking at ten months. I mean, look at me. . . ."

Failures are nothing more than information. Directions. Go this way. No, not that far. Back that way a little bit . . .

Think of failures as directions, and try to get more—more information, more help, steering you toward what you want.

With respect to doing what you are meant to do with your life, this is the most important thing to keep in mind. There are millions of people who get up every day and fight traffic to get to a job they don't particularly like. They spend their day around people whom, if they didn't work with them, they'd have absolutely nothing to do with. They work for money that may or may not be all that great, for so many hours a week it leaves them no time for anything else. When you ask them how they got into this dilemma they say, "Oh, I competed for the opportunity."

I am no longer impressed by people who do work they like, but I am fascinated by people who consciously do things they don't like—and the world is full of them. It's full of people who go after jobs they don't want. It's the only area I know of where people suspend, over and over again, total common sense. "I got a job doing something I don't like, I'm working with people who drive me crazy, and I picked it." It would be like marrying someone you can't stand, or buying a house in a neighborhood you hate. There are no other precedents I know of.

When my oldest daughter was four, we were playing and she said, "Daddy, did you know that drawing is my most favorite way to play?" And I said no. We kept playing and talking, and then eventually I had to stop because I had a client coming. My kids have grown up with clients coming in and out of the house, so it was no big deal. But I saw the opening, and I took it. I said, "Daddy has to stop because I have a client coming. Do you know why Daddy works?" And she said, "Yes. So you can make money to buy food and toys." And I said, "Well, that's one of the reasons Daddy works. But the main reason I work is that this is *my* most favorite way to play."

So often when my clients tell me work is not their favorite way to play, it's because they haven't bought into a fundamental truth, which is that our lives are made up. If you are making it up anyway, why not make it up so it's fun?

My job is to help people get effective lives, and I use myself as an example. It never made sense to me that you had to work five days a week. Why five? People used to work seven days a week; then they worked six and a half, then six, then five. So I said to my brain, this is the deal. I am going to earn a living and I'm doing it in a maximum of four days a week. Three and a half would be good, but four days max. Now get going. Get working on it. Those are the parameters.

I didn't want to hear anything from my brain about five days, because I wasn't going there. It had to be three and a half to four days, because I have other things I want to do—like really be there for our three children. That's what I wanted, and that's what I got. All my energy went into making it happen.

It boils down to this: Are you or aren't you going to participate in your own life? You can be in the parade, or you can sit on the curb and watch the parade go by.

The people who don't really want to participate in their lives have bought into the lie of status quo. They think that, left unattended, things stay the same. But that's not true. Left unattended, things get worse. You cannot opt out of your life. It doesn't work. You can get in your life and be in the parade, or you can sit on the curb. But you can't do nothing. A decision to do nothing is a decision to voluntarily let things get worse.

One other thing: Don't make the mistake of thinking that reaching the goal is the goal. Going for the goal is the goal. If you don't enjoy getting there, you're not going to enjoy being there. Constantly telling yourself that you'll enjoy life someday when this or that happens is just a variation on keeping your dreams distant. Do whatever you have to do to be as happy as you can, right now.

There is a life in the balance.

Chris Shea

LIFESIGHS

The first person I ever showed my greeting cards to was a florist, a very successful florist in San Diego, where I live. I took the cards in and waited for the owner. He was busy attending to something else, but finally he sidled over to me. I put my eight little designs on the counter in front of him and he just looked at them. Then he looked at me and said, "*This?* This is your idea of a card?" Then he walked over to a rack of cards he had in his store and picked up one of them, a big, huge, fancy-schmancy card. He walked back over to where I was standing and practically shoved the card in my face. "This," he said, with great aplomb, "*this* is a greeting card. This is what people who come in *here* are looking for." He gathered up my cards at that point and kind of tossed them back at me. I was heartbroken. Heartbroken. I went back out to the car, put my head down on the steering wheel, and cried.

I composed myself after a few minutes, put the key back in the ignition, and went on to the next place. It took me months to find an account. When I did, I bought two boxes of envelopes—250 per box. Now I buy many thousands at once and have them delivered, but back then, 500 envelopes were a lot. I remember thinking, if anyone sees me coming out of this paper store with all these envelopes, I could just tell them that one box was for me and one was for my mother.

The cards caught on. A sales representative for another line noticed my cards were selling and asked if he could represent me—and eventually he did. We now have more than 300 styles, and that includes Christmas. When a given style does not sell, we retire it. My employees say the card is going to the farm now, and I always hate to say good-bye when one has to leave us.

The cards are shipped all over the country. I'm surprised at how well the business is doing, but then again, I'm not.

I always knew I could write. I had written a column for a little local newspaper, and I knew I had writing skills. I also knew I had art skills, which—although they weren't phenomenal—were enough to escort the words off the page and into somebody's brain.

I think I always also knew that greeting cards were something I could do. I started making them when my kids were little. I made them and gave them away, and people liked them. So I knew it was a talent that people had an interest in. But I almost got into the business on a dare. I needed a job, and I wanted to start a greeting card company—someday. And my friend said, "Well, why don't you start the company today?" I told him that wouldn't be possible because my youngest son was, I think, just twelve then. And he said, "What's your excuse going to be when your youngest son is twenty?" It made me mad to hear that, but it also made me think, "Well, why not?" So we went downtown and I took out a business license, got a post office box, and started drawing cards by hand. And that was that. That's how Lifesighs Cards began.

I look at it this way: You just have to go where you feel like you're being led to go. And what you wouldn't have done yesterday, or what you might not do tomorrow, might be the consummately perfect thing to do today. I think you always have to listen to what is right to do now. That's key. It's that whole *now* thing.

There were times when I thought, what the heck am I doing, but I'm coming to this conclusion in my life: that there really are two parts of us. There's the part of us that knows there is nothing, absolutely nothing, we can't do. But then there's the louder part of us, the part of us that never shuts up, that constantly, for some reason, wants to protect its own smallness. And the more you exercise being bold, the more you start to quiet that nagging, doubting voice. And that's what enables you to just think, *I absolutely can do this.* Even though part of you might be thinking, oh my God, I hope I can.

As to what my life means, there's probably one moment that speaks the loudest. It was when I got a call from a woman who wanted to know if I sold greeting cards to individuals. I get calls like that all the time, and usually

I say, no, we don't. But she was a very pleasant woman, whereas a lot of them are kind of rude. So this time I said, "As a rule we don't, but is there a particular card you're interested in? We could probably locate it for you from a store and have it sent to you." And she said, "Well, it's that card that says, 'God knew they couldn't afford announcements, so he lent them a star.'" I knew the card she was describing. It was a Christmas card with a drawing of a big long string and a great big funky-looking star and these two sheep looking up at the star.

So I said, "Oh, I know I can get that card for you. I'm glad you like it. It's been out for a while." And then she told me her son, who was sixteen, had committed suicide that past summer. Now this was early December. I told her I was so sorry. And she said that at his memorial service, the minister referred to him as a star who was lent to us by God. She told me she hadn't wanted to send out Christmas cards because it felt disrespectful to him. But then, when someone sent her that card, it was as if it were him telling her to send out cards—wanting her to celebrate Christmas.

Of course, I asked her how many she wanted and sent those off as a gift to her and her son. I combed through all my other stuff to find other cards she might like. I packed the box and sent it off, and I still hear from her, off and on.

I think this is really the reason there is such a thing as Lifesighs. The concept has nothing to do with anything originating in my head. I think it originates in a place that's common. It's just that I happen to have my radio tuned to hear it. So when I put a sentiment down on a piece of paper, somebody else has already felt it, they know it, so they see it and they recognize it. Lifesighs has a very juvenile sort of style that I think resonates with people because it reflects memories we all have of something good.

It's not just my work, either. I think everybody has an opportunity to say something, to give something to people that moves them in a way that far exceeds the actual apparent reason for doing it.

People wonder where I get my sense of peace, and all I can say is, I listen. That's the main thing I do. A lot of people call me an artist, which I never think of myself as being. I consider myself a writer, but if I had to pick a job title it would be listener. Sometimes coworkers will walk by my office to find me just sitting there. "Catching things?" they'll say. "That's exactly what I'm doing," I answer. I'm just listening to what goes on around me. And then I know what to write. I know what to say to the people in my life. I know where my heart wants most to go.

It's like right now. My assessment of the reason I'm enjoying this conversation so much is because I'm completely invested in what I'm telling you. I'm not distracted, or thinking, oh, I forgot, I have to do . . . whatever.

That's what makes focusing on what's in front of you so intoxicating. You're in the pure act of living. That's the goal, to figure out how to keep yourself living right now, as opposed to viewing your life through the fears of the past, or the dread of the future, or the opinion of somebody who thought you were stupid. Because that all comes in, in that loud other voice. If you can quiet that voice, you can give rise to another one—and learn how to really live.

Nancy Solomon

FEAR SEEKER

My dream was always to become a psychotherapist, but my family did not approve. I joke that they were afraid I'd find out how dysfunctional we were. Eventually I went into the fashion industry. Nothing to disapprove of there—I come from five generations of fashion-industry executives. And I started climbing. I kept earning more and more money as I became more and more miserable.

This went on for eighteen years.

At the eighteen-year point I was traveling a lot, and I came back from a trip and sat on my couch in my apartment. I looked out the window and realized my view was of another building. You'd think I would have known that already, but that's how little I was home. My view was of a brick wall.

I looked at that wall on August 21, 1991, and I said to myself, "That wall is symbolic of my life. How much money are they going to have to pay me to make me forget how much I hate my life?"

I sat with that question for a while. When you ask something like that, you can't go backward and unask it. The question's been asked, the universe hears it, and you can't just pretend nothing happened.

Within four months, I was fired from my very important job. I don't know how many people who, in the moment they're being fired, think, "Yes! There is a God!" But I did. It wasn't that I knew what was next. I drifted for a few years. But eventually, when I asked myself what I really wanted, I had an answer. I want a house on the beach. Check. I want a dog. Check. I want to go back to school and study psychology. Check.

I went into practice as a psychotherapist and really enjoyed it for about eight years. Then I adopted two children and now make my living as an executive coach, consultant, and human potential expert. I'm doing some writing and public speaking—whatever terrifies me the most at the moment. That's because I'm starting to think there are two kinds of fear. There's red-alert kind, telling you to back off because you're going to get in some kind of trouble. And there's the kind of fear you run toward because you're about to have a breakthrough.

It's not that I can always tell the difference. What about when the answer isn't obvious? Here's what I tell people: "Choose failure over regret. And rejection is God's way of saving you the trouble."

Barry Levenson

MUSTARD MAN

Did you hear the one about the attorney who opened a mustard museum? That's me. I was a lawyer for more than fifteen years, and had a great job as law jobs go. I got to argue before the United States Supreme Court, and in some ways it was very fulfilling work. But there was always a part of me that wondered what else I could be doing with my life, and I didn't want to look back and have regrets.

I can remember the exact moment I decided that I didn't have to take the safe route through life. It was October 27, 1986, just after the Boston Red Sox lost the World Series. I was a depressed Sox fan, having grown up in New England—even though I was living in Wisconsin. I went to an all-night supermarket because I couldn't sleep and roamed the aisles, figuring I needed some kind of hobby to take my mind off my depression. When I was in front of the mustards I heard this voice that said, "If you collect us, they will come."

People think I'm making that up, but I'm not. That's exactly how it happened.

I think the fact that my father was a small-business owner had something to do with my not being afraid. I knew the kind of commitment it took.

Over the next five years my mustard hobby became an obsession, and I eventually left law to open what is now the Mount Horeb Mustard Museum. It has the world's largest collection of mustards. There are almost 5,000 on display, and we also have a retail shop and mail-order catalog.

I think what surprised me the most about my new life is how many people share my passion. There aren't very many of them who would have taken the risk I did, from what they tell me, but I think they admire me for pulling it off. And that feels good. The biggest joy I get is seeing the smiles as people peruse the shop or the museum. As an assistant attorney general, I wasn't used to dealing with a lot of happy people.

You hear the expression, do what you love, the money will follow. And I'm here to tell you that doesn't happen overnight. It may never happen. But I've learned that there's a whole lot more to life than how much money I'm making. There are times I look back wistfully at the years of someone else paying my health insurance. Then I remember what it felt like to go into the office every day, and even though I didn't mind it, I wouldn't trade the sense of satisfaction I have now for all the money in the world.

I feel like I did something creative with my life. And every time someone calls 800-GET-MUSTARD—sorry, I had to work that plug in—I feel like I'm doing what I was born to do.

Malcolm Bryan

TWENTY-FIVE-YEAR PLANS

Oil painting was my major in college. Okay, it wasn't just my major. It was my life. I wanted to do that for a living, but my professors said it wasn't possible. They said the only way you could make a living as an oil painter was if you were a professor. And I believed them.

So I sold out. For twenty-five years. I was twenty when I made this pact with myself. No matter what I was doing when I was forty-five, I would quit that and start painting. I figured by then I would have saved enough money to take the risk, but I didn't want to make it any later because I wanted to make sure I had the energy to pull it off.

I became an air freight forwarder, eventually owning my own company. I was the middleman between the shippers and the airlines. It was a lot like being a travel agent, except you handle freight. There's a lot of pressure, a lot of competition, and it's a very cutthroat business. But it provided well for my family, which made it difficult to tell my wife I was going to keep the promise I'd made to myself when I was twenty.

I made the switch six months before I turned forty-five. I'd grown weary of the lifestyle, and the Stapleton International Airport where I was based was going to be replaced by Denver International—which was a very inconvenient thing for the air freight industry. I didn't want to be around for that. So I thought, well, now's the time.

We moved to Gateway, Colorado, which is something of a misnomer because it's fifty-five miles from anything. I started painting there. Eventually I moved to the town of Grand Junction and met some successful oil painters who taught me that you could make a living at this work. I went to art shows and met other people who were succeeding at the profession, and gradually I gained confidence that I could too.

But it took much longer than I expected. I had this idea I could sell my work to the general public at low rates in the beginning, and that was just totally wrong. When I started, I couldn't sell it anywhere. It took me three years after I began painting full-time to get my work into a gallery. So, for three years, I not only wasn't making any money, I was draining my savings.

I guess what kept me going is the same thing that keeps anybody going if they believe in something, just persistence and tenacity. I felt I had the talent, but needed to learn how to make it a business.

People say, "Don't you wish you had started right out of college?" And I shrug. I developed so many business skills in my former life and I matured as a person, two things I think are key to the success I'm having now. A lot of artists never acquire business skills, and no matter how much you think you're just going to go off to a studio somewhere and paint, the fact is you're spending a lot more time selling than you ever dreamed. Even if you're prepared for that aspect, as I was.

So it has been more work than I ever thought it would be.

It has also been more fun. In twenty-five years it would be easy to idealize something so much that the real thing could never live up to that version in your mind. But it has exceeded every expectation. The process of learning how to paint has surpassed my wildest dreams.

When I was in business I was always very conscious of time passing, of time running out. Now I feel that time is endless, because I'm so immersed in what's right in front of me.

I am at peace, moment by moment. My life is a work of art.

THREE

Stop

A Kansas farm couple needed some extra money. "We have to sell what we have," the man told his wife. "We don't have anything," she replied. "Okay, then let's sell that," he countered. They decided to rent out a couple of vacant farmhouses to hunters, and placed this ad in the *Chicago Tribune:* "If you want to get away from it all, we have the place for you. We're about as far away from anything as you can possibly get, and there's absolutely nothing to do here."

"And, by golly," the man reported, "we got a call from this guy in Chicago who said, 'That's exactly what we're looking for.'"

—Darrell Anderson, *Successful Farming Radio Magazine®*

I went to the *Parachute* workshop because I had come to an important intersection in my life and wanted to be careful before I crossed the street. Stopping at that intersection was the best present I ever gave myself: two weeks to dwell on a single question, "What is the absolute most fun you can imagine having for the rest of your life?" Once I brought that vision into focus, there was no going back.

We did a lot of exercises, reflecting on what had worked in our lives and what hadn't. Mostly we focused on what had worked. We wrote seven stories about things we'd done that we felt really good about. We picked the stories apart, decided what skills we most loved using, and figured out where we'd most love to use them. The man sitting next to me wanted to know what my dream job is. I couldn't even say it out loud, it seemed so out of reach. I just scribbled r-a-d-i-o in his notebook. "Oh, you'd be *perfect* for radio," he exclaimed, and told me why.

I knew before I got to the workshop that radio would be as much fun as I could have. Even in grade school I wanted to be in front of a microphone, giving speeches or doing readings. I forgot about that as I grew up. Work was just that: work. It wasn't meant to be fun. So I studied engineering, worked in management and sales, and hated every single minute.

But always, always there was a weatherman in the back of my mind. I'd read about him in a magazine when I was a teenager. There was such glee on his face in the photograph! He was standing under an umbrella in a downpour.

Printed on the umbrella was: "See, I *told* you it would rain!" And get this. He loved his job so much he was embarrassed to get paid for it.

To love your job so much you're embarrassed to get paid for it! I couldn't get over that. But now here was *Parachute* author Dick Bolles, systematically proving to us that we're meant to love our work. Suddenly it was okay to take my dreams seriously, and it was exhilarating.

Dick saw me smiling during the first exercise and offered this reassurance: "If you're not having fun you're not doing it right." I knew he wasn't just talking about the workshop. He was talking about life, and I had approached it backward. I thought you were supposed to work hard, save a lot of money, and if someday you had the luxury of having fun, well, good for you.

It never occurred to me that life was supposed to be much fun until "someday."

I was wrong.

Realizing that changed everything. Had I not stopped for a few weeks in between jobs, I might have missed it.

I think I would have made the same career change without the workshop, but probably would have second-guessed myself all the way. Instead, by pausing at this crossroads, I marked some big lessons. The most important one being that who I am and what I love doing is not a mistake.

I was realistic about the time it would take to start over in something completely different from the sales and management track I'd been on. I waitressed at night to pay the bills, a job that did not impress. What was I doing mopping floors and stocking bar glasses? For the first time in my life, I didn't worry about what other people might think. That was the biggest gift from the workshop, a quiet confidence about what's right for *me.*

It didn't take me long to find a job selling advertising for a radio station in St. Paul. Getting a sales job was like taking everything I learned in *Parachute* and setting fire to it. That's my style too, though—get a recipe for success and then not follow it. I didn't take the direct path to a dream job; I meandered a little. It's like my friend Cliff Hakim remarked about his career: He had a plan, but "everything happens on the side streets."

George McDonald

WILLING AND ABLE

I run a company that helps homeless men and women get jobs—and addresses. The program is Ready, Willing & Able, and it's a part of The Doe Fund. It's holistic, and it takes twelve to eighteen months to complete. People get trained to go to work, work hard all day, get along well with others, remain drug free—and come back tomorrow and do it all over again.

I was in the apparel business for fifteen years and got tired of stepping over the homeless in doorways on my way to another $200 dinner. I decided to do something about it. My Catholic upbringing is at least partially responsible. I can still hear the nuns telling me, "Other people's miseries are your miseries."

The Doe Fund, which I founded, is named after a woman we called Mama Doe. I used to feed her in Grand Central Terminal in New York, and she died of pneumonia in 1985—the year I set up the fund.

We have hundreds of trainees in Ready, Willing & Able at any one time. Since 1990 we've helped more than 3,000 of them become drug free, get full-time jobs in the private sector, and secure their own self-supported housing. In the beginning, about a fourth of graduates still had jobs three years later. Now it's about three-fourths.

My guess is that when most of us see a homeless person we don't think of them as a parent. But two-thirds of our trainees have between one and seven children. So Ready, Willing & Able is also changing the cycle of dependency and poverty. It saves tax dollars, sure, but it also saves the costs associated with crime and violence.

It's beyond my wildest career dream to run this organization. The thrill! To help people who are the most difficult to serve in society—to help them prosper in our free enterprise system. That's a great accomplishment and the satisfaction is daily. There are ripples, too. We do street maintenance in Manhattan, which is obviously good for the city, but it's also a great way to keep the word out about our program. You can find Ready, Willing & Able in Jersey City and Philadelphia in addition to New York. Our graduates find work in mailrooms and restaurants and hotels and hospitals, as well as many other institutions. We've won awards for what we do in and for communities.

I know a lot of people who work at a job all day that means very little to them, so they try to squeeze meaningful experiences—like volunteer work—into the scraps of time left over. That was okay for me too, for a while. Then I realized there was too much work to do, and it was time to be part of the solution.

Mike Lenich

MAKING A LIFE

I always thought the secret to life was making more money. It took me a long time to realize the secret to life is spending less.

For twenty-four years, I worked for an electric company in Chicago. I started out sweeping the floor in a generating station and ended up as a quality manager for a division. It became apparent in the early 1990s that your job wasn't necessarily secure anymore. It used to be that you'd go to work for a utility and that was it. Unless you really slipped up, that was your employer for life.

The biggest thing I learned during my time with the electric utility is that the more money I made, the more I spent. I felt trapped. Then I read the book *Your Money or Your Life* and started keeping track of where the money was going. I had no idea I was spending $40 a month just on coffee to and from work, for example. I had all these subscriptions to magazines I didn't have time to read. And so on. So having this new understanding of where the money was going made it easy to get rid of unnecessary expenses. My wife and I eliminated a whole lot, things we thought were making us happy, but really weren't.

As our expenses started to come down, we started saving money—and the savings began earning interest. Nothing fancy. Just common everyday interest from thirty-year bonds.

It was almost like we turned our financial life on its head. Instead of seeing how much stuff we could buy, we started seeing how much stuff we didn't need. We got real focused about it, and then something unbelievable happened. In December 1999, the interest from our bonds started to exceed our expenses.

I didn't need to work for money anymore.

It was exciting, but also scary. I was forty-five, and I'd been working a long time. The first thing I did was pick up my guitar again. I hadn't played it much since I was a teenager, and I missed it. I discovered a whole series of venues here in the Chicago area where you can grab a guitar and participate in what they call a sing-around. You sit in a circle and everybody has a song. It doesn't cost a thing, and you get to meet a lot of people. A few of us started a band, and I've been playing ever since.

A typical day for me is getting up early and taking a nice long walk or run. Then I come back and meditate. Then I play the guitar and teach some lessons. After that, I might have lunch, walk up to the community center and visit with friends, spend some time at the library, whatever.

My wife and I coordinate a simplicity group that meets the second Saturday of each month, and I volunteer to do income tax returns for the elderly through the AARP from January to April.

Just walking around town is a treat. For more than twenty years, I never saw much of it. I'd get up at four-thirty, be out the door at five-thirty, and not get home until seven. Now the pace of my life is much slower, and I don't feel as if it's passing me by. I like to tell people that I made a living for twenty-four years, and now I'm living.

Sally Hogshead

RADICAL CAREERIST

I've always had a radical career. You could say I'm a radical careerist. I'm the breadwinner in my family and once took a 50 percent pay cut for the sole purpose of working with smarter people. At the time I was running my own advertising agency, dealing with clients I'd pitched and won and created successful advertising for. I had employees I'd recruited from around the country and I had an amazing business partner. I was leading a very profitable, secure business and I got bored.

This was a calculated risk. I was opening the West Coast office of Crispin Porter + Bogusky, the hottest agency in the country and maybe even the world, working with people who knew how to do things that very few people do. Opening day? September 10, 2001. The venture failed, and most of the reasons were beyond my control. But I learned some important lessons as a result, and I marked those lessons in a book, *Radical Careering*.

I gave a lot of thought to my mission in life after the book came out. At first I thought my mission was to sell a lot of books. That was exciting for about two weeks. Then I realized my goal wasn't so much to sell books as it was to empower people to create careers they passionately love.

One of the most important things I learned through this transition was that you have to live in verbs. You can't just sit there waiting for a situation to get better. You have to pick yourself up and actively plot the steps to get you where you want to go next.

Another thing I learned was how important it is to be the dumbest person in the room sometimes. It's not what most people I know aspire to, but think about it for a moment. If you surround yourself with morons, you're not going anywhere. You're not getting pushed and challenged, you're not learning anything, you're playing on the C team. It's only when you put yourself out there wholeheartedly and are willing to feel stupid for a while that you'll make the big leaps. That's why new jobs are scary. That's why people often shy away from them.

It's kind of a shame, really. Instead of getting more comfortable with mistakes as we get older, we grow more fearful. The problem is, if you don't continually give yourself permission to fail, then in direct proportion you're not giving yourself permission to succeed. The greatest successes require some degree of risk, and by definition risk means you could fail.

The question is not, "Are you going to fail?" Failure's a part of life. The question is, "What are you going to learn?" I bet if you make it a point to surround yourself with people who value failure you'll be in the company of tremendous successes. Failure isn't the opposite of success. It's part of the package.

It's an art, really—failing successfully. Make it a point to laugh about your latest failing over drinks with a friend. Celebrate it. When I interview people, that's one of the first things I want to know. "Tell me about something you failed at and what you learned." If they aren't willing to admit they failed, or worse yet, haven't put themselves out there enough *to* fail, they're probably not big enough thinkers for me to want to hire them.

Failure's like a muscle. You have to keep it strong. You need to have small failures constantly to keep you in shape for the big ol' whopper that comes along once in a while. Let that failure muscle get flabby and watch your life unravel. You won't have that strength of character that resilience brings.

I have resilience, and that's why I didn't consider myself a failure when I realized that even though I was a career coach and a motivational speaker, I no longer loved what I did for a living. I was spread so thin I became the person I talked to in my seminars and wrote about in my books. I knew I needed to take action, but didn't know what action to take.

So we stopped.

My husband and I sold our 4,000-square-foot house in Los Angeles and moved into a tiny apartment in Jacksonville, Florida, with our two kids. I took a sabbatical from much of my career so I could focus on getting back to what it is I love. My husband is a stay-at-home dad, and because I'm pulling the wagon it's very important for me to be successful and love what I do so I can keep doing it effectively.

The step we took was radical by any standard, but it allowed me the space to breathe and figure out what I most wanted to do next. Don't think that having written a book about living radically means it was any easier for me. I still have the same realities anyone else does, all the trappings that come with modern life and all the responsibilities that can drag you down.

I think if you don't know what to do next, the first thing you should do is stop.

When your computer freezes, sometimes the only option is turning the darn thing off and starting over. That's what I did in my life. I hit the reboot button.

Then I went back to my first love, advertising. I love to empower people, and have learned not everyone wants to be empowered. But almost everybody wants to sell more product and make more money, and I'm good at that. So while I'm still writing, I'm also a creative director. I work with start-ups as well as Fortune 500 companies on their ad campaigns. I'm a speaker and consultant too, but I've returned to my core—advertising—for inspiration.

Steve Simenowitz

SYRUP IN MY VEINS

I have maple syrup in my veins. My wife and I bought a tree farm in Vermont, which just happened to have a mature sugar bush. True to form, I shot the hole and painted the target around it, and that's how we got into making maple syrup. Rather than impose my dream on the farm, I let the farm tell me what it wanted to be.

I've always been interested in organic farming, but for a long time we were about as far from that life as it is possible to be. I was an attorney and my wife was an executive. We were living on Long Island and had six-figure incomes. We had a staff. We had lawyers and para-legals and gardeners and nannies and housecleaners, and one day we realized we were no longer in control of our lives.

One day I went to a workshop entitled "Getting By on Less" and this man stood up and said, "We subsist on $6,000 a year." I thought to myself, "That wouldn't get me to the fifteenth of any given month."

So we quit our jobs and moved to the country, pretty much just like that. And the first thing I learned was how much I had to learn. They don't teach you small-engine repair in law school. But there's an excitement about being a total novice, and you do gradually learn. It's thrilling to find you can survive in an environment totally foreign to you. Plus the stress of a runaway horse is nothing compared to the stress of a runaway client. Although I will say that just because you're living in the woods doesn't change the fact that most businesses fail. People don't realize how much money it's going to take to get going, and they go under before they can.

Having said that, how much money you have in life is not a function of how much you make. We were making insane amounts of money on Long Island, but we were spending it just as quickly. It's much more about your cost of living. My car insurance has gone from $2,000 a year to $200. My mortgage up here is less than my taxes were on Long Island.

I can live richer on a lot less, and that's a secret that passes a lot of people by.

I also can honestly say I love my life. We give new meaning to the phrase "niche marketing." We bill ourselves as the only Sabbath-observant, organic, kosher, horse-powered maple syrup farm. Someone turned us on to the idea of selling not just the syrup, but the trees—so we started an adopt-a-tree program. It's a nice, high-end gift item. When we sell a tree, at the end of sugaring, the customer gets a gift box with syrup and pancake mix.

We savor every drop of syrup. It's packaged in high-end glass bottles. We even developed an exotic line of numbered, signature-series bottles—we take the first production run and sell it under a private-label name. There are some people who want to buy into that magic, the same way you'd buy a $60 bottle of Scotch.

We sell eggs. We have an egg business called The Heavenly Yolk, and we actually paint little yarmulkes on the eggs.

We also have in mind a point beyond which we don't want to grow anymore. Otherwise you don't really own the business. You're back to it owning you.

What I love about my life is having time for things like ag-education programs. I go to local schools and try to reconnect kids with the food supply. We bring chickens and show the children where eggs come from. They visit our farm and see all the ways we try to save water, so that maybe when they get home they'll be less inclined to crank the faucet when they're brushing their teeth.

I think of it as leaving a softer footprint upon the earth. We're trying to make the world a better place, one pint of syrup at a time.

Janice Lasko

ROADIE

I flunked retirement.

My husband and I decided we were finished with Los Angeles when I was in my early forties and he was in his midfifties. We moved to a little town in the High Sierras in California. I'd been working in advertising and my husband was in construction sales. We both took early retirement and applied for only those jobs that would allow us to ski during the day. We knew we wanted to do more traveling as well, so we bought a recreational vehicle.

We took small trips to begin with. The first one was a whopping seventeen miles from home. But we wanted to get to know the RV before we took it on longer trips.

It wasn't long before we spent more time traveling than we did at home, so we decided to try it full-time. We went on a two-year test drive, so to speak, and rented our house.

We thought we were going to be all alone out there. We had no idea we were about to join quite the community of mobile street people—or affluent street people, depending on who's talking. So we weren't exactly pioneers, though not to hear the people closest to us tell it. I'll never forget sharing with our best friends our decision to sell the house after all. The women took me into one room while the men stayed with my husband.

"Normal people," they told us, "do not abandon family and friends."

What could we say?

"We're not normal."

We just really wanted to head out on the road. We set goals. You know, serious grown-up goals like, "Ski at every resort in the country."

We've been living and working in an RV for twenty-one years now, and we've been having so much fun. I started editing *Escapees* magazine several years ago—and do it all from the road. I feel like the luckiest person alive. Everything is from a new vantage point with every issue of the magazine.

It is a different life. You know what I miss about being in a house? Corners. When you live in a house you can make a left turn, a right turn; you can go into different rooms. In an RV you just go up and back, up and back.

Life in an RV is quite the escape from the slow march toward whatever it is we call the golden years. Though there are small things you can't escape, like laundry, and people you can't escape—like your partner. It always amuses me when a couple decides they're going on the road to solve their problems. Going on the road won't solve anything except the scenery.

I love this life. There's something very pure about it. You don't fall into a trap of accumulating possessions, because there's no place to put them. You rely on your ingenuity to make money—as opposed to staying in the good graces of an employer. And you're definitely choosy about the battles you pick with your traveling companion.

You know how you get to a certain age and all people want to talk about is their aches and pains—and where they went on vacation? Being an RVer doesn't spare you the aches and pains, though they do seem to be fewer with this lifestyle. But you don't have to spend your waking hours daydreaming about where you'd rather be. You live in a vacation.

FOUR

Ask for Directions When You Get Lost

There are a lot of people around who will tell you what you *should* want from life. . . . You don't have to accept their answers. Ban the word "should" from your job search.

—David Maister, *Savvy*

The biggest mistake job hunters and career changers make is looking for advice in all the wrong places. That's according to Dave Lorenzo, a consultant and the author of *Career Intensity*. Lorenzo says you see it all the time. You're at a picnic, and your Uncle Joe pulls you aside to tell you it's all about computers. Never mind you have no interest in or aptitude for computers. People can't wait to tell you what fields are hot. As if that has anything to do with what excites you.

"I work with a guy," Lorenzo says, "who's unbelievably successful. He's the top salesperson in his company and he sells forms. He essentially sells paper. He sells checks, he sells prescription pads, you name it. He makes a fantastic living, and for the last fifteen years people have been telling him he's in a dying business. They tell him computers are going to make paper unnecessary. He listens and nods, then goes back to work and makes more money."

Lorenzo's in the advice business, but people have offered *him* plenty over the years. "I have two master's degrees," he says. "Why do you think I have two master's degrees? Because somebody told me it would be a great idea. I didn't need all that time in school to do well in my profession. But somebody gave me the advice that this was the right thing for me to do, so I did it."

The world may or may not be your oyster, but it can certainly be your classroom. Want balance? Find people who are doing a good job juggling their many roles, and take notes. Do you want meaning, happiness, a sense of adventure? Find people who live with passion and take more notes. Or keep reading!

Dick Bolles

USE YOUR GIFTS

As the author of *What Color Is Your Parachute?*—the best-selling life-planning book—I'm often asked what the secret to happiness is. This is my answer: Use your gifts. They have a kind of energy, and if you don't let that out you will go crazy.

I think of a cat that came to our house for the first time. It was an adult cat and we wanted to train it, so for a week we kept it in the house before we'd let it out into the yard. We didn't want it to run away, or to run back to where it had come from. And during that week the cat was going nuts, because it would go up to the windows and see all these birds out there. It wanted to be outside, it couldn't be outside, and it was driving us nuts along with it.

Finally the day of freedom came for this cat. He was able to go out into the garden, and you have never seen such happiness.

I think our gifts are like that. They don't like to be caged up inside of us. They like to find expression and they like to get out there into the world and be used.

You start out by seeing that each of us has been given two gifts by God. The first gift is that we have been given certain talents. We are able to do certain things. I knew a woman who could walk into a room where there were twenty people seated around a table. She'd look at them all, turn on her heels, and walk out of the room, and she could perfectly describe what all of them were wearing. Just like that. Jewelry, watches, hairdos, everything. She thought everybody could do that. And I told her, they can't, I guarantee it. But how would she know? You don't walk down the street saying, by the way, if you walk into a room, can you describe everything you saw?

So oftentimes, people have skills that they didn't even know were skills, because they thought they were just normal things everyone can do. Many of us were given skills that are so innate to us we don't even stop to count them.

The second gift we're given is a love of certain of those skills. I can raise money—I used to do it when I was a pastor in a church. The church had a monetary goal that needed to be raised. I would make 300 percent of that goal, but I had no taste for it. I didn't like to do it, and eventually I got out of doing it. So we have to ask ourselves, why is it we like to do certain things and don't like to do other things? Even though I'm gifted in some areas, I still have my personal preferences for skills I like to use and skills I don't. It's been my experience that you love to do certain things because God gave you the gift of loving *that.* That's how he indicated to you what he wanted you to do for him and for the world.

So God gave you certain gifts, more than you need, but he gave you a love for the ones that he most wants you to use. And that's how we divine what it is we're supposed to do with our lives.

You may have a gift that other people have, but you also have other gifts, and it's the way you string those gifts together, much like beads on a necklace, that makes you *you.* It's what makes you unique among all the people who are on the face of the earth. Discovering those gifts and giving the world what it needs most—what only you can give it—I think is just absolutely the key to happiness.

Dave Swanson

GOOD QUESTIONS

What do you want to do with your life?

As a young man, my answer to that question was, "I want to work with people." I went into advertising and later became the personnel director at Manpower, which I enjoyed. I was also assistant director of admissions at Northwestern University. Both jobs let me explore the field of career planning from the other side of the desk, and I learned a great deal. Now I counsel people about finding work they love—and when I ask them what they want to do with their lives, almost all of them say the same thing I used to say: "I want to work with people."

I suppose it's a way of keeping our options open, staying somewhat vague, and it was only after meeting Dick Bolles that I realized career planning doesn't work that way. I went to one of Dick's three-day workshops in 1975 before I had even read his book, *What Color Is Your Parachute?* In three days, he turned my view of the world of work upside down. I used to think you just tried a lot of different things and hoped one of them stuck. Now I know better. You get to know *yourself* before you worry about where you fit in the world. Take the time to create a clear, detailed picture of your ideal life. *Then* go find it.

As a career consultant, I'm fond of asking people to complete this sentence: I have to _____. I often think of George Balanchine, the famous ballet director, who was quoted as saying he doesn't hire people who want to dance. He hires people who *have* to dance. What is it you absolutely have to do on this earth to be happy? Then do that. Employers love to hire people with passion.

Career planning is not a process that can be rushed.

The first thing I tell anyone who calls me for advice is this: Don't be in a hurry. If you've been out of work for a while and the bills are piling up, I can understand the urgency to find another job. But young people, for example, think they have to decide what career they'll be in for the rest of their lives, and think they have to decide now—or else. Or else what? "I have to do this fast," they'll tell me. "I'm twenty-eight years old!" Pause. "In two years I'll be thirty!" I don't know whether to offer them an energy drink or a cane. But that's youth. Kids want to be everywhere all at once. They have to talk to their friends every five minutes, and they have to load their iPods with 5,000 songs. Five thousand songs! I have a few hundred CDs, but I bet a third of them are still in the wrapper. I don't have time to listen to them.

There are some things worth doing slowly. Career planning is one of those. People spend forty, fifty, sixty hours a week at their jobs—for forty or fifty years! Isn't it worth some time to think about how to make that time—your life—enjoyable?

One thing I loved about interviewing people for a living was how much I learned that I could pass along to the next round of candidates, and now to my clients. I've always been struck by how unprepared most people were when they came in. They didn't know much about our company, they didn't know about the competition, they didn't know enough about anything to ask good questions, and they didn't know how to present themselves.

The biggest mistake they made was not dressing up enough, believe it or not. This is the simplest of things, and it trips people up. It keeps getting worse, too. Showing respect—by being prompt, sending a thank-you note, or dressing for the occasion—is almost passé. Want to set yourself apart from the competition? It's easier than you'd believe. Use common sense. No, your resume doesn't have to be one page. But make it readable and not book length. I have a resume from a twenty-seven-year-old that's twenty-six pages long. If I haven't listened to some of my CDs, I'm not going to read about someone for twenty-six pages.

You must zero in on what you want. You have more skills than you can count. Use the book *What Color Is Your Parachute?* to prioritize those skills. Rank them. That list is magic. What is the number-one thing you have to do to be happy? You now have a target. It's much easier to hit a target if you have one.

People think they increase their odds of finding their dream job if they stay open to anything. The opposite is true. Ask college students who are about to graduate with a business degree what they plan to do with it, and I'll bet their answer will be, "I'm going to see what comes up."

Let's say we're talking travel as opposed to career planning. You're lost, and someone offers to help. "Where do you want to go?" he asks. And you say, "Anywhere is fine." He'll probably just stare at you before walking away. But if you tell him where you want to go and point to that location on a map, he can help. He *wants* to help.

Figuring out where we want to go is a painful process for some of us, because we may have to accept we've done "the wrong thing" with our lives so far. Or we may realize big changes are in order and we don't know how to summon the courage. You just have to ask yourself if you really do want to be happy. There isn't necessarily a recipe for that. You won't know the answers in advance. But where would the adventure be if you did?

Kaile Warren

SAY A PRAYER

I used to build houses for a living. Ironic, isn't it, when you consider I later became a homeless person? In 1993 I was in a bad car accident that kept me out of work for eighteen months, and my life started to unravel. I went broke. I got divorced. Things kept getting worse and worse, and eventually I was sleeping in an abandoned waterfront warehouse in Portland, Maine. You'd think I would have been praying long before it got to that point, but I wasn't. Until this one night I just asked. I asked for help.

I woke up at three o'clock the next morning with an idea: Rent-A-Husband®. I would do the jobs that husbands never got around to doing. Fast-forward to the present, and . . . talk about a present! Rent-A-Husband has thirty franchises throughout the United States. We're looking to open 500 more over the next five years, and have expanded overseas with franchises in England. I do the home repair segment on the CBS *Early Show* on Saturdays, I've written a book, and I've appeared on *The Oprah*

Winfrey Show. That isn't the best part. The best part is how I feel, on every job, watching some customer's face light up at the thought of having her chores done. It's often the smallest thing that can drive you crazy, after all, like a leaky faucet. "You may charge $50 an hour," women will tell me, "but I think that's really cheap for a good husband."

You want to talk about someone without regrets, you have come to the right place.

In the past seven years, I have never once felt like I was going to work. I love every minute of the day. I tell people that on Sunday afternoons, I almost can't wait to go to bed so I can wake up and it'll be Monday morning. How many people do you know who feel that way about their jobs?

I love how my story is unfolding, but it never really got interesting until I hit bottom. So I credit the bad times for the good ones, definitely. And while some people say it doesn't take much courage to go after a dream when you're in my situation and don't have any alternatives, I disagree. I learned from the bad times, and the biggest thing I learned was to have the courage to hang in there.

That served me well as I started dreaming big—really big, as corny as that sounds. I think courage, more than the hardships I've had in my life, is what sets me apart.

I meet a lot of people who are passionate about something, but that's where it stays. You tell them to go after their dream and they'll find a million reasons why they can't. It's like they have some stake in things remaining just okay, or worse. It's like they're afraid of success.

I was afraid too. I had failed before and knew I might again. Here's how I got over it: I found something I was more afraid of. And that was dying with regrets. Dying knowing I could have had a wonderful life, but was too afraid.

Lucy Kaplansky

FACING THE MUSIC

I'm a full-time singer-songwriter. I tour all over the United States and Europe, and I love my life.

I started out as a singer and decided to quit when I was in my early twenties. I went back to school and became a psychologist. I probably would have been perfectly happy being a psychologist had I not gone into therapy myself. I needed help to realize my passion really was music and I was just running away from a whole bunch of conflicts I had with it. I was crazy *not* to pursue it.

In retrospect, there was definitely a fear of failure. I was afraid I'd find out I wasn't all that good, and one sure way to avoid that is to not even try. But there was also a fear of success. I've always had a hard time letting myself have what I want. Singing was the career I wanted most, and denying myself that felt like the right thing to do—for a while.

We tell kids to ask for directions when they get lost, but for some reason when we grow up we think it's a sign of weakness. I think it takes courage to ask for help, and it's one of the best things I ever did for myself.

Not that some of my fears weren't well founded. It takes years to get established in the music business. I started in the late seventies and think the recipe—if there is such a thing—has two ingredients: talent and perseverance. If you're good, people hear about you. So you go and do open-mike nights, you go do opening acts, whatever, and word starts to get out. I've seen that with so many people and that's what happened with me. But it takes years. It took me years to make a name for myself. When people ask me for career advice I tell them if they're good, everything will work out—if they put themselves out there enough.

My music isn't easy to describe. I suppose you could call it a combination of rock, alternative country, folk, and pop. It doesn't fit neatly into any genre at all, which is okay. I think we get too hung up on labels, not just in music but in life.

I'm becoming more well known all the time, it seems. I had back-to-back hit albums, *Ten Year Night* and *Every Single Day,* that each received the AFIM (Association for Independent Music) award for best pop album of the year.

My heart was in music from the time I was a very little kid. It's always been obvious to other people that I wanted to sing. I love it. It's in my blood. There was a lot of music in my family, and this path was a natural.

I think the biggest mistake people make when deciding what to do with their lives is focusing too much on the world outside rather than the world inside. Consider the successful people you know, or know about. Chances are, if you interviewed those closest to them, they'd tell you the signs were there from a very early age. It makes me wonder if in the process of growing up we forget who we were as children. And that to really *be* a grown-up—a happy one, anyway—we have to go back and find that person.

Joan Baker

JOAN THE VOICE

I didn't set out to be a voice-over artist. I wanted to be an actress. I got into voice-over work because it's a career I couldn't be seen in. I'm biracial. My father was white and my mom's black. So there's always been the question of what category I go in. That's a big thing in show business. What type are you? The people in charge worry that if you're watching a commercial and I'm in it, you're going to spend thirty seconds trying to figure out if I'm black or white, rather than focusing on the product. Not my thoughts, though.

As an actress, I had trouble getting an agent. It seemed like I could never catch a break. Feeling particularly low one day, I flipped through *Back Stage* and noticed an ad for a voice-over coach, Joni Robbins. Her first name was the same as mine and something clicked. I decided to do a voice-over tape, but only because it might be another way to get myself out there.

Joni helped me create a demo with cartoon and character voices—which I'd always been good at—and added a couple of sample spots with my normal voice. I encourage people to have someone direct their demo because it's almost impossible to be objective about yourself.

Once I had the tape, I started at the top talent agencies and was going to work my way down, but I didn't have to. The first day I got into a top agency. The man started listening to my tape and within seconds told his secretary to hold all his calls so he could listen to the rest of it. I walked into another agency the same day and got another interview. The third agent I spoke with was Don Buchwald—he represents Howard Stern—and that's the agency I signed with. I've been working steadily ever since. My client list reads like something straight out of your wildest career dream: American Express, ABC News, HBO, ESPN, Sony Music.

I'm the exception, in terms of how easy it was to get started. But I'm like any other voice-over artist in that, even though we have agents, it's still up to us to find work. An agent can get you auditions, but you have to get the jobs, and you're always looking for the next one. Even if you have a contract with a television network, there's no guarantee. Producers change positions, and the new ones like to bring in their own people, so you're back out there looking.

People say to me all the time, "I've been told I have a great voice and I should get into voice-over." As if that's all there is to it. If I wanted to be an accountant, I wouldn't apply for a job and say, "Someone told me I'd be good at this work." I'd go to school and find out for myself. As a matter of fact, in the voice-over industry your voice isn't even all that important. What's more important is how good you are at marketing yourself, how well you take direction, and how consistently you make the copy you are reading come to life.

I can understand the fascination with my work, though. It *is* fun. I love it. I love the freedom of expression. I'm reading what someone else wrote, but if what I brought to the message wasn't important, the writer would be in front of the microphone. I love inspiring people, informing or entertaining them.

I also love coaching people in voice-over. Your voice is a blueprint of who you are. I can tell from the way someone breathes what her issues are. Children breathe with their diaphragms, the way we teach professionals to breathe, but they do it instinctively. As they grow they accumulate fears and blocks, all of which are reflected in the voice. Then I think we spend our adulthood trying to get our breath back, trying to recapture the wonderful way we had of looking at the world. Which is why, when you see someone doing work she's meant to do, you say she's found her voice. That's exactly what has happened.

Voice-over work helped me find my voice, too. I took a class on self-expression and leadership, and we had to do a project that would impact the community. My father had recently died of Alzheimer's, and one of the cruel things about that disease is losing the ability to communicate.

I created a book, *Secrets of Voice-Over Success,* in the class and started working the phones. I talked with top voice-over actors about how they made it in the business, what advice they have for others, and how they'd like to be remembered. I also included in the book a section about Alzheimer's, written by professionals—explaining what the disease is and how you can help. All my royalties benefit the Alzheimer's Association.

Writing the book and getting it published gave me a new appreciation for letting go. By that I mean, the more I try to control what happens, the less it seems to go that way. Let's face it, your career in show business is at the mercy of a lot of people, which can make you neurotic. You may as well surrender to the magic of not knowing how things will turn out.

I'm starting to enjoy that.

Margaret Riley Dikel

WHAT'S NEW

I call myself an information consultant. I guide people to information that can help them with their job hunt. I got into the research field by way of research. I was working as a university librarian when somebody asked me one day if there was anything out there that could help him find a job. I put together a list of resources that would become *The Riley Guide.* It started as a ten-page print handout of about twenty places on the Internet where people could find job listings—primarily in the sciences and in engineering. That was late 1993. In 1994, we put our first guide on the Internet, and it wasn't long before we stopped producing the print version.

The Riley Guide is what's called a gateway site. There are approximately 5,000 links to resources for job hunters, career information, how to prepare for the world of work, how to write a resume, and how to handle a difficult boss. I'm picky about what resources I list. There has to be something you can use without getting charged up front. If you go to a website and all it's doing is selling you a book and it wants your credit card information before you can see anything, forget it. That's not my idea of a useful resource. At least give me a chapter to look at so I can decide if the book is worth my money.

A lot of people say *The Riley Guide* is the best place to start your Internet job hunt, and I think one reason is that I keep it simple. Someone who is new to job hunting or the Internet can get around pretty easily. I spend a lot of time making sure the information is current, and sometimes it can be overwhelming. Once in a while I step back from it a bit. I don't think you can be in the business of sharing career advice if you let your own career grow stale.

So I try different things. I'm the creator of a virtual career center for the National Institutes of Health and enjoy that very much. People who work at the NIH generally get six- to eight-year fellowships and then they have to find other jobs. There was a big need for the career center and we came in under budget. I had to laugh. When I became a private consultant, my father asked me what will happen after everyone in the world knows how to search for a job. I told him I don't think that's going to be a problem.

I think in the beginning people were hopeful the Internet was going to be the answer to their job-hunting problems. It certainly seemed that way in information technology. All of a sudden the demand for people with IT skills was exploding, and it was natural for employers and job candidates to find each other online. That was an unusual time, and not something the rest of us could count on. Even people in Web development can't rely on the connectivity of just the Internet anymore.

The biggest mistake people make when looking for jobs is spending too much time in front of a computer when the most effective networking happens in person. I think the Web is a tremendous resource for career information. Applying for jobs online isn't necessarily any more effective than using the classified ads in a newspaper. What you can find online consistently is information—about employers, the skills and qualifications employers are looking for, salary surveys, things like that. It used to be a project to research a company. You had to go to the library, of all places, and check many sources. Now there's no excuse for walking into an interview unprepared.

One of my favorite things to do online is learn what different kinds of jobs there are in the world. Things you would never think of, like forensics. It's not just what they do on *CSI*. There are forensic accountants. Those are the guys who track the money back ten years when you suspect the CFO has been bilking your company. I'm trained as a librarian and you could think, well, I can work in a library—or a university—and that's about it. False. Records management is a wide-open field right now, and librarians are well qualified for those types of positions.

Not only do you find job titles you might have never thought of, but chances are it will take you only a few seconds online to get a firsthand account of a day in the life of someone doing that work. There's your information interview, and you haven't had to pick up the phone. Of course, the article may point to an e-mail address, so you could correspond with that person for more information—or find out when he or she will be attending a meeting of a professional association in your area, so you start networking in person.

What I love about my work is the unique window it gives me on life. What could be more exciting than reporting on the world of work? Librarians are like scientists in that they're trained to love the questions. Every day my job is to find out, "What's new?" And then tell you.

Bobbi Miles

INNKEEPER

Sometimes the task isn't to ask for directions when you get lost. Sometimes you have to take getting lost *as* your direction.

My husband and I have grandchildren scattered around the country. We like to visit them a lot, and Bruce is a pilot, so we spend a lot of time in the air. Summer of 1999 we were on our way to Denver, where we live, but had to turn back toward St. Louis because of a storm. We knew we needed to land right away and saw a very small runway, which was fine. We have a small plane and don't mind small runways. After we landed, we went to the little phone inside the terminal and called the police to find out we were in Smith Center, Kansas. We didn't have a car, so the cops came out and took us into town. We ate lunch and stayed at a little bed-and-breakfast there.

The weather kept us in Smith Center for three more days. People were really nice. The owner of the bed-and-breakfast loaned us his Cadillac so we could travel around and see the area. We had always wanted to buy and re-model a Victorian home in Denver, but they run almost a half a million dollars. That's before you gut them and put all kinds of money into their renovation. So when we came across a Victorian home in Smith Center for a frac-tion of what they were going for in Denver, well, let's just say we were intrigued.

The weather cleared, we went home, and that was going to be that.

Later that summer as we flew back home from St. Louis, we ran low on fuel and had to stop—guess where—in Smith Center, which we were prepared to write off as a co-incidence. Until a little later that same year, when we had trouble getting fuel and were several hours behind schedule. We didn't make it all the way back to Denver before dark. Can you guess where we stopped again? Yeah, Smith Center.

Fine. This was meant to be, we said. We bought that old Victorian home and spent the next winter vacationing, if you can call it that, in Kansas. Whenever we had a few days free, we flew in. We gutted the house and spent every minute of our spare time fixing it up. By the next spring we realized we were working in Denver, but living in Smith Center. We made a deal. If either of us got a job in Smith Center, we'd sell everything we had in Denver and start over in Kansas. And just like that, my husband, who teaches shop in high school, was offered two jobs in our new hometown.

Since we had gutted the house we bought, we had no-where to live. We approached the owners of the bed-and-breakfast on the outside chance they were interested in selling it, and they were. Now we had a place to stay, and I had a job too.

We loved it from the beginning. We love the community, we love running the bed-and-breakfast, Bruce loves his teaching job, and I love devoting—and dividing—my time to both our new home and the bed-and-breakfast. We get up early and fix breakfast for our guests, and Bruce heads to work while I chat them up. You have the most interesting people passing through. Each one of them has a wonderful story. Sometimes we take them over to show them the progress on our home, if they're interested in that sort of thing.

At one point early on, the gas bills at the inn were so high that I had to get another job to cover the difference, and I became director of economic development for the city. I'd get things straightened up at the inn, then drive to work. It was a whole forty-five seconds away. In Denver the commute was forty-five miles, one way.

There was a lot of travel in my new job, but very flexible hours. I was good at it. I think the people who hired me thought, "Who better to sell others on moving here than someone who made that decision herself?"

In a former life I was a research scientist and was used to exploring new territory. I had been working at the University of Colorado. I was a late bloomer. I went to college when I was thirty-two and kept going until I had my PhD in analytical chemistry, specializing in atmospheric chemistry. I spent more than five years with the National

Oceanic and Atmospheric Administration, then another six years running a research group at the University of Colorado in Boulder. I went to international meetings and, with the aid of a translator, set up a research station on a Korean island. It was very exciting stuff.

But Bruce had summers off, teaching high school, and he had an airplane. I loved to fly because I'd done research out of planes. We decided it would be nice for me to have summers off, too. I left the university to teach science at the same high school where Bruce worked. They were in desperate need of science teachers in inner-city Denver, and I could make more money teaching high school for nine months than I could in a whole year doing research at the university. Then we landed in Smith Center three times that one summer and thought, "We need to pay attention to this sign." The grandkids were arriving, and I realized I was one science teacher or scientist out of millions, but I'm one of just two grandmas for my grandchildren. It wasn't a difficult choice to make. Changing careers would mean more time for family, period.

People look at me at work at the inn and want to know why I'm cleaning toilets when I have a PhD. I shrug. I don't really mind it. It's enjoyable, a vacation from the stress of running a business and everything that goes with it. Doing simple things like cleaning bathrooms is soothing.

If you're lucky enough to pass through Smith Center, I invite you to stop by the Ingleboro Mansion. I'd love to show you why I can't imagine being anywhere else.

FIVE

Accept Free Samples

> Adults are always asking kids what they want to be when they grow up because we're looking for ideas.
>
> —Paula Poundstone

It took me several weeks to decide to buy a $4 pretzel. Every other Saturday, browsing the mall and savoring still another mouthwatering sample, I contemplated my choices. There was quite the array. Eventually I settled on Parmesan, with honey mustard on the side.

I spent more time deciding on a pretzel than a college major—another reason I wound up with a degree in engineering. Lucky for me, I also had three internships in school—construction work, railroad design engineering, and manufacturing plant management—so I knew for sure by the time I graduated I wanted nothing to do with engineering.

I was sold on internships, though. The chance to try on a job before you signed up for full-time employment—why wouldn't you do that? Well, okay, the pay isn't usually very good if you get anything at all—and most people have to do other work to support the supposedly free trial. But to sample a new job before committing to it? Truly, in my opinion, priceless.

You don't necessarily have to be a student to intern, and there are other ways of sampling careers. Do volunteer work. Help a friend whose work intrigues you on the weekends. I know people—and you'll meet a couple of them—who tried on a new career just by entering a contest. My first sale as a writer was a twenty-five-words-or-less essay, submitted for a "Back Home for the Holidays" contest sponsored by *Good Housekeeping.* I said I wanted to go back home to Minnesota because my new husband has never looked out the window of a "Mary Tyler

Moore" house and watched kids playing hockey on a frozen neighborhood lake. I didn't win the grand prize, a trip back home—but I won a dishwasher. As a feature-writing teacher pointed out, home is where the dishwasher is.

"It doesn't surprise me that you won," a friend said. "It surprises me that you entered." I thought about that for a long time. Haven't you always wondered who really wins those contests? It didn't matter. The fun I had putting that sentence together! You can have your dishwasher and the home that goes with it. I just wanted to keep writing.

It was in the feature-writing class that I learned the power of a good letter. After turning in one assignment, the instructor asked me to help him with a book. Now *that's* an internship, I remember thinking. This opportunity might take me somewhere I actually want to go. I'll never forget one weekend afternoon, helping Vince. I was using the same computers real writers used to file real stories—heaven. I wasn't getting paid, unless you count the appreciation from someone who became a good friend—and the chance to work on something that had meaning for me. "I could spend my whole life at a sales job," I told him, "and never get the satisfaction I'm getting from my tiny part of this book."

I interned to get into radio, too. I worked at the Minnesota News Network (MNN) in St. Paul. I didn't spend all day wishing I was doing that kind of work, because I was finally *doing* it. No one pulls you aside to tell you that you're too intense. You're supposed to be intense. I had found my people.

Going into radio—or writing—means taking vows of poverty, at least to begin with, at least in my case. When I interned at MNN, I barely made enough from a waitressing job to pay my rent. But I was happy. I didn't even know I was happy until a friend took still another job as a sales rep—which wasn't exactly her calling, if I'm remembering this right. "I want a nice life," she told me. That part I remember for sure. Because my next thought was, "I'm glad I got *that* out of my system. I want an interesting life."

We try on clothes, we test-drive cars. When the stakes are higher—forty or fifty or sixty hours a week for maybe decades—we might do ourselves quite the favor by approaching our careers the same way.

Cyrus Nowrasteh

SCREENWRITER

I won a Kodak young filmmakers' award when I was a junior in high school. I think the prize was $50 or something—which might not have covered the speeding ticket I got racing to the awards ceremony. The film was just this goofy little western set on a friend's ranch. But we shot late in the day, in what's called—as I found out later—the golden hour. So we had some beautiful shots that probably made up for a rather simple story.

I was hooked. I went to New Mexico State on a tennis scholarship for my freshman year in college but transferred to the University of Southern California (USC) when I got accepted to its film school. USC was great because it's right in Los Angeles and a lot of people from the industry either teach there or speak to students as they show off their new films. Steven Spielberg came to one of my classes.

I taught tennis after I graduated to make ends meet, but I wrote like a maniac. I just sat down and wrote movies. That's how you break into the business. You write screenplays and try to attract the attention of an agent. Agents are hounded by thousands of writers running around with screenplays under their arms and, well, good luck. It's one of those things where, if you knew how difficult it would be, you might not have the courage to set out. But I didn't know, and eventually I got an agent.

Having an agent doesn't mean instant success, not at all. I didn't make a dime from screenplays until I'd written ten of them. Along the way I was lucky, sure, but I think more of my success has to do with sheer, dogged persistence. I've worked on TV hits like *Falcon Crest*, but if you've heard my name lately it's probably for the ABC miniseries *The Path to 9/11.*

I write constantly. Not everything sells and not everything works, but every few scripts or so you come up with a gem—and when that happens, people get excited about you and your work. You have to stick with it and keep writing whether they're excited or not.

I love the high I get from working on a script I think is really good. And even for successful screenwriters that feeling is rare. A small percentage of what gets written makes it into production.

People think I have a dream job, and in some ways I do. It's not as glamorous as you might guess. Sure, sometimes you're on set or in production meetings with Hollywood types, but mostly I'm sitting at home in front of my computer. Then again, that's probably the best part—I'm not waiting tables hoping to get a screenplay produced someday. This is my day job.

Leigh Anne Jasheway-Bryant

THE ACCIDENTAL COMIC

A lot of people in the comedy field had a plan. I was not voted class clown in high school. I was voted most likely to depress people. In my thirties I discovered how much humor could help me communicate. I was a health educator, trying to talk people into eating better and smoking less and doing other things that are good for you. I just kind of stumbled on the idea of using humor to inspire them.

I accidentally took a comedy-writing class, to tell you more of the truth. I was going through a divorce and someone said, "You need to do something fun." So I opened up one of those adult education catalogs and selected something at random. It turned out to be comedy writing. That's why I'm the accidental comic. The man who taught the class told me I had talent and encouraged me to take the stand-up class. That's where I learned that being funny isn't about telling jokes. It's about using what happens in your life to tell stories. The more embarrassing the stories are, the better.

On my second day as a health educator at the University of Texas, I fell out of a van in the parking lot and broke my arm and had to file for workers' compensation. Two days later I'm sitting in my office chair pecking away on the typewriter with my good hand and I hear my new boss calling me, wanting to tell me something. I can't hear her, so I back up thinking I'll get closer, not realizing she's standing right behind me. I roll over her foot and break her toes. This story makes the point that when you get off on the wrong foot, so to speak, you can still have a wonderful time. I was in that job for twelve years and loved it. I taught aerobics on the side and wove humor into workouts to distract people from the fact they *were* actually working out.

Not everyone can do humor, but I've been teaching comedy writing and stand-up for thirteen years at a community college in Eugene, Oregon, and most of my students don't want to be comedians. I've had bank loan compliance officers and educators and school bus drivers and nurses and therapists and unemployed people. Everybody who's taken the class has become better able to use his or her sense of humor, so it *is* something you can improve.

I think the worse your experience in life the funnier it will become as the years go by. I tell people it's a shame to wait years to laugh about it. Start laughing about it as it happens. There's a life skill.

I drove from one side of Oregon to the other on my way to a big presentation recently. There aren't many public bathrooms through all those mountains, so when it was time to heed the call of nature, I did so up against a big tree. I got back in the car and realized almost as soon as I started driving again I must have scraped my backside on that tree. I didn't have time to check it out, so I kept driving—and by the time I got to my destination I'd forgotten about it. I was in the buffet line with the people who were going to listen to my speech when a giant piece of bark fell out of the back of my pants and landed on the floor next to me. We were all looking at it, but I was the only one who knew what it was. This is the moment at which most people would have prayed for the earth to open up and swallow them, but I let out a sigh of relief and said, "Thank heavens. Now if I could just get the squirrel out of my pants."

I won the Erma Bombeck award for comedy writing with my true story about how my first mammogram caught on fire. Now I help judge that contest.

I go into organizations and show people how to use humor to diffuse stress and build teams and enhance creativity. I make up games and use music.

They say laughter is the shortest distance between two people. But here's the thing: To make someone laugh, especially someone you don't know very well, you have to be a good listener. It's a connection, not a one-sided communication. When you make it, when someone cracks up at something you say, it's better than taking a bath or eating chocolate or taking a bath *in* chocolate.

Did you know little kids laugh hundreds of times a day? Then they get to school and it drops way down. They start being told, "Grow up, get serious, act your age and not your shoe size." I think the most harmful thing to tell a child is, "That's not funny." It also doesn't make sense, because you're telling him that something is not funny when he's laughing—so obviously it *is* funny. And you're setting him up to believe he can't trust his instincts. I tell adults in workshops and conferences, "You are not the god or goddess of comedy. The only person you get to choose what's funny for is you."

I don't care what your job is, there's nothing to lose by lightening up. That's another thing I teach in my seminars. If you can't remember the last time you laughed at work, if you can't imagine a time when you'd be able to laugh at work, maybe it's time to get a new job. I tell employers, all other things being equal, hire the applicant with a sense of humor. You can usually teach computer skills. You can't make a person fun to be around.

What is my best advice for your career or life in general? Make funny friends. I have a friend who is really big. One day we were waiting in line for supposedly fast food but it was taking forever. The poor girl behind the register apologized to each of us, even though it wasn't her fault. Finally it was Nick's turn to order. "Sir," she said, "I am so sorry about the wait." Nick looked at her. "Honey," he said, "I've weighed this much for so long it really doesn't bother me anymore." These are the kind of people you want in your life. They not only make you laugh, they show you the light. So make lots of funny friends, even if you have to stalk them first.

Derek Evilsizor

FRANK SINATRA

I used to repair copy machines for a living. I had plenty of time to indulge my passion, which is karaoke. I entered a lot of contests. My life changed when I won second place in a nine-week, big deal competition in Denver. My prize was a karaoke machine, which helped me start my own karaoke business. Then I got discovered, just like you hear about in the movies. A guy from New York was in town and heard about me. He came into the bar one night and said, "You look like Frank Sinatra. Why don't you get yourself a suit and meet me at this little wine bistro next Friday?"

I bought the suit, thinking it would be the worst $200 I'd ever spend. I showed up ready to sing some of Frank's songs and used the karaoke machine as a crutch. People liked it. "Come back next week," the owner said, "but leave the machine at home. I don't want karaoke."

I hardly slept that week while learning about thirty Sinatra songs.

I got the job. Friday and Saturday nights, I became Frank Sinatra. There were probably forty people at my first performance, but soon a hundred or more were cramming into a place that had an eighty-six-person capacity.

I'll never forget one night early on. I walked through the door and everyone stopped to look. "Frank!" they hollered, and started clapping. I got a standing ovation *before* my show. My girlfriend and I both cried and I said, "This is it. This is what I want to do."

My reputation continues to grow. People tell their friends to come and see me. "You can't believe how much he looks and sounds like Frank," they say. I perform for 1,500 people, and at private parties in houses so big I could fit my own house in their living rooms. I used to make $15.50 an hour fixing copiers. Now people get out of Ferraris, watch me perform for an hour, and tip me $100.

I try not to let it go to my head, but it's heady stuff when you're used to office work. One thing wasn't a struggle— wondering if I should take the risk. I didn't look at it as a risk. If this didn't work out, I knew I could fix copiers again.

I take life as it comes. Ask someone who's seventy years old what the point of it all is, and the answer will often be, "Don't worry about it. Just enjoy yourself." When you're young you think old people are blowing you off, like it's some secret they're keeping to themselves. Then you get a little older yourself and you realize, "They're right. That's it." Just have fun, and don't worry about things too much. If you're having fun, you're probably doing the right thing with your life.

Laura Hutchens

MEDIA MASTER

I stumbled onto my dream career by volunteering. I was my sister's ride to a meeting about a cable program that was starting up in my hometown of Dayton, Ohio. I hung around for the meeting, and by the time it was over I was hooked. This was back in the early days of MTV. Everyone was excited about this local version—geared toward kids—of a music video program. I volunteered to help and eventually got a job at the station. I produced the show, met my husband, and the rest is personal history.

I was just out of high school and didn't have a clue what direction I wanted my life to take. I was interested in biology, but didn't know what I could do with a degree in it. I remember sitting in that meeting and thinking, "This sounds like so much fun." I was still enough of a kid to also think, "Well, why not? Why not do something fun with my life?"

After my husband and I graduated from college, we spent some time in Atlanta working for Turner Broadcasting.

We grew up in the production departments as those networks grew up. I was with the Cartoon Network in its infancy. I'd tell people, "I get paid to watch cartoons." There was more to it, but that *was* part of the job.

After a while we decided to go into the production business ourselves and started a company called Curious Cumulus. My business card said writer-producer, but that didn't begin to cover it. I wrote scripts, sure, but I also shot and edited video, swept the floors, and in some cases rewired the editing suite. Pretty much anything my clients needed me to do, really. I soon learned what being in business for yourself means. You have creative control, but the price tag is brutal. You almost have to train for a pace like that. We were lucky to find corporate clients in Dayton, where we returned after working in New York for a while and making valuable contacts there too. I can't tell you how many times we worked twenty hours a day for several days straight. Then production wrapped on that project, we took a day off just to sleep, and started all over again on another equally brutal job.

One aspect of the work I loved was the access to people I would have been too shy to approach otherwise. In high school I wasn't even bold enough to order my own food in a restaurant. This business cures you of that quickly. I've done work at the United Nations and I've met Lena Horne, for starters.

The other thing I loved was the freedom. I was the person planning my day. I could make almost as much money as I wanted, depending on how many hours I could handle.

If we wanted to stack projects close together, to make room for scheduling time in Canada where my family has a place, we could do that.

Fun has been such a reliable compass that I continue to use it as I chart the next move. Right now I'm teaching media in high school and love that too. Every year I get a whole new batch of kids who can't wait to learn everything I can teach them about TV, radio, animation, and Web design. It's the best. I get to pass along my passions, and they inspire me daily.

Perhaps the greatest thrill is being asked for advice. I feel qualified to offer it because I came to teaching by way of the "real world." I tell students, with confidence, that the best way to discover what you're good at is to try it out. You can't know if a field is right for you by reading a course listing in a college catalog or a classified ad in a newspaper. You have to give it a spin. I hammer on the importance of internships and job shadowing. As kids come back to me in later years, which I hope they'll do, I'll say the same thing. If you're unhappy, do something about it. You don't have to be in college to intern. Call it volunteer work or community service. But it's a great way to sample a new life before you commit to it.

I do it all the time.

Steve Feinberg

PERSONAL TRAINER

I always thought I'd be a psychologist. My friends in high school used to call me at two o'clock in the morning for advice about what to do about their troubles. I drifted some in college, and got into sales after that. I enjoyed sales. It was fun.

One day I was waiting for my friend Vito to get off work. I wandered by a martial arts school and watched two guys doing some of the coolest things with their bodies I'd ever seen. One had a spear; one had a shield and a sword. They were doing a two-man fighting set, and it looked like a Sunday afternoon television movie.

I wandered in and asked a couple of questions. They told me to come back another day with more appropriate clothes and try out a free class, which I did. I loved it. I signed on that day. It was the first time I ever put something on my credit card, and I was pretty excited.

It wasn't long before they offered me a job as assistant program director for the school. I put the usual effort into that, which is to say everything I had. My boss liked what he saw and called me in for a meeting. "You're going to run my school now," he said. "You're my new program director. This is how the job works. . . ." It wasn't even a question. It was just, "This is the deal."

Soon afterward, I got another call from the boss. He was running late and had a client waiting for him. "I'm not going to be able to make it on time," he said. "I need you to do this private lesson." Although I was terrified at first, I jumped at this chance, too—and loved it. There was a real sense of satisfaction working one-on-one. So I got certified to teach and started training clients at some of the most elite health clubs in Manhattan. Eventually, the time was right to start my own business.

Now I'm running a company called Speedball Fitness. Speedball's a unique cardiovascular program that adds a medicine ball for resistance. A Speedball class is almost like tai chi, sped up. Your abs will feel it for days, but if you give it a chance you'll get hooked on it, I promise. Our program's being picked up in schools and we've been featured on national TV shows like *Queer Eye for the Straight Guy.*

I have employees and all the business details that go along with that, but I've kept some private clients. I can't live without the personal connection. I got into this business because I wanted to motivate people, and no matter how successful we get, I want to keep doing what I love the most.

One thing I'm fierce about is keeping my personal fitness routine fresh. That's why my clients respect me.

They see me stretching in more ways than one. A while back I took up boxing. I had the chance to train a top-ten-ranked athlete, which was a thrill. When it was time for the big fight, my client knocked out his opponent in three rounds, and I couldn't have been more ecstatic if I had been the one throwing the punches.

I'm constantly asked what the secret is to staying in shape. All I can tell you is what you've probably heard before. Showing up is 75 percent of the battle. Hire someone like me, or just make a deal with a friend that you are going to meet at this time on these days of the week to work out. Make those dates as sacred as taking your kids to school or showing up for work.

This is a dream job in too many ways to count. I'm locked into being fit, for one thing. It's impossible to have any credibility if I'm not in perfect condition myself. The main reason I love the work is for the chance to be part of the solution to a growing problem. I've seen the same news reports you probably have about the obesity crisis in this country. It's a great feeling to know I can help change the situation. I'm doing my part to make the world a better place.

Mark Greenig

WOODCARVER

I'm in charge of community education in Detroit Lakes, Minnesota, but my passion is woodcarving. I make duck and fish decoys out of wood. I deal with people all day long in my regular job, which is fine. But it's nice to go home and retreat to my shop. Just the aroma of the wood is soothing.

I learned the basics of woodcarving in a community ed class I set up in 1985 and have been at it ever since. It's such a joy. Sometimes I don't even carve in my workshop. I just sit in it. You'd have to see the room to believe it. It's filled with decoys.

I'm always upgrading my shop. I barter for all my wood— I trade duck and fish decoys for it. But the rest of my hobby gets expensive. It took a few years for my wife, Lois, to come around. I keep telling her this is part of our retirement portfolio. If I ever have to unload any of it, I'll be able to. It only increases in value. You wouldn't believe what people pay. I have to laugh when I hear someone tell a child it's tough to make a living as an artist. What I do is art and it commands serious money. Just like for other art objects, there's a collectibles market out there.

I recently bought three empty boxes for antique spearing decoys—those wooden fish I was talking about—and the total came to $65. The containers are harder to find than most of the decoys but will often more than double the price you can get for the decoy alone. To someone who isn't as into the art form as I am, which is to say almost everyone, $65 for three empty boxes seems like a lot of money. "Are you nuts?" is more how Lois puts it. She just shakes her head.

My trouble is letting go of something I've created. I do it for fun. When someone gives me an order, it becomes work. There are deadlines and there are requests to do it this way or that, which takes the fun out of it to some extent. I'm still learning how to blend passion with business.

I teach classes on woodcarving and I always tell people, "Carve the way you want to carve. Paint the way you want to paint. You have enough people telling you what to do in other areas of your life. You probably have a boss, maybe a spouse and children, each with different ideas of what you should do in the course of a day. When you're in your woodshop you're the boss." I believe that's what a lot of people are looking for. A place they can retreat to and have fun. If you have a hobby, you'll probably be a lot happier. I am, anyway. I am a better employee, husband, and father for doing something I find enjoyable. I have something else to look forward to, another reason to get out of bed in the morning.

Let's face it. Jobs change. Kids grow up. Don't wait to discover what you love to do—paid or unpaid—until your golden years. If you don't have a hobby by the time you retire, it may be too late. Someone once told me you can't just retire. You have to retire into something. I believe it. I can't wait to get older. I'm having a great time already, and the future holds even more promise.

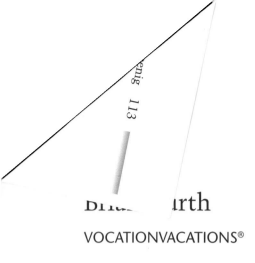

Brian Kurth

VOCATIONVACATIONS®

Nothing against the Kennedy Expressway in Chicago, but I longed to hit a different road. It wasn't that my corporate job was so bad. I just thought there had to be more to life than being another lemming following a career path lacking passion or fulfillment.

So I took six months off to travel, and spent much of that time just asking people what they did for a living. And I was struck by how many of them apologized for that. "I went to law school," they'd tell me. Or, "I made it through med school." And then, "And now I have this thing I have to do for the rest of my life." There wasn't a lot of sparkle in their eyes as they talked.

Then I'd ask what they really wanted to do. Once in a while, they would shrug and say they didn't know and didn't care. They are the kind of people for whom work really is a four-letter word. But most people had a dream. "I'd train dogs" was something I heard a lot. Or be a professional gardener. Or open a winery. The list was endless.

"So what's stopping you?" I'd wonder. And much of it was just the fear of the unknown.

It got me to thinking. What if you could test-drive your dream job the way you test-drive a car? Just take it for a spin. It struck me how many of us probably spend more time deciding what car to drive for the next three years than what career to work in for possibly the rest of our lives.

I turned the idea around in my head. What if you could live your dream job for a few days on an otherwise traditional vacation? You wouldn't have to tell your boss. You wouldn't have to quit your day job. You wouldn't have to leave the security of what you're doing today.

Welcome to VocationVacations.

VocationVacations is a company that helps you sample a different life. You may love it so much you'll move the mountains—of obligations, of family and friends telling you you're crazy—to go get it. Then again, you may not. Isn't being an innkeeper, for example, the most romantic-sounding thing, until you're scrubbing toilets? Being a winemaker is dreamy too, until you're schlepping case after case into a shipment truck. And owning a bakery? I hope you like getting up at three in the morning. You get the idea.

The concept caught on, and now I'm as busy running this company as any of the corporate types I left behind in Chicago. But my days are filled with meaning now: helping others find meaning in their work too.

SIX

Say Yes

> I will not die an unlived life. . . . I choose to inhabit my days, to allow my living to open me, to make me less afraid, more accessible; to loosen my heart until it becomes a wing, a torch, a promise. I choose to risk my insignificance.
>
> —Dawna Markova, *I Will Not Die an Unlived Life*

It's one thing to say yes to a dream. That's easy. It's saying yes over and over and over, when the world is saying no, that will take you where you want to go.

Think of any experience you cherish. I bet it started it with a yes and not a no.

The first week of my sophomore year in college depressed me. I knew by then I hated engineering—hated it. And I had at least three years of school left. I didn't know what to do. The thought of quitting turned my stomach. I don't quit things. But by then we were into the more difficult classes—and I wasn't going to be able to fake my way to a degree. No partial credit for essay questions. You either solved an engineering problem or you didn't. There were a few professors who gave you some credit if you got partway to the solution, but I had trouble making it that far.

Now what?

I thought back to spring semester and a talk given by a favorite professor. I trusted him and listened intently to his advice. "It's about now," he said, "when a lot of you will want to quit." No kidding. Engineering students, as a friend put it, were dropping like flies. At some level I knew there's no shame in quitting, and I was allowed to change my mind. "Before you do," the professor suggested, "make sure you're running *to* something and not away from it."

Bingo.

I got my degree. I didn't know what the heck I'd do with it, but when you don't know where you're going, you may as well hang out where you are.

What about you? Are you saying yes, or saying no?

Jane Brody

CASTING DIRECTOR

I'm a casting director. I'm a member of the Casting Society of America, a designation of which I'm very proud. I was an acting teacher in Chicago at my own studio, The Audition Center. You always think of actors being discovered, but casting directors can be, too, and that's what happened to me. A casting director from New York saw me teach a class and thought I'd be good at casting. The idea intrigued me. So when an agent called one day and asked if I'd try it—the local casting director, she said, wasn't seeing all the talent in town—I said yes. That's how I got started.

The first commercial I cast was for a bank. We had to go into several neighborhoods in Chicago and find the face of each neighborhood. So I had to find the face of the Polish neighborhood, the face of the Italian neighborhood, and so on. I loved it. I loved it right away. You have to be a good researcher in this business, and that's something I love to do. I'm kind of a history nut. I've traveled a lot, and I love to explore the world.

I know within two seconds of meeting someone if that person is right for the part I'm casting. I've cast the films *Fargo* and *Groundhog Day,* some of the movies that Oprah has made for television, and almost too many commercials to list. I make quick decisions. It isn't so much about saving money as it is about trusting your instincts. Sometimes I'm surprised—in other words, I may change my mind and go with someone I wouldn't have after the two-second mark—but not often. This business is all about trusting your first impression. You know how your mother told you not to make snap decisions? Well, I was bratty and I made them anyway. That's part of what makes me good at this job.

Think about it. It doesn't take you very long to decide if you like the person you're watching on TV, for example. You either take to the kid in the oatmeal commercial or you don't, and you do that right away. Casting for those commercials is honoring how the audience will react. Whatever its reaction, it will be quick. It makes sense to cast that way.

I cannot imagine tiring of this work, no more than if I tired of life itself, because I get such a fascinating window on the world. I've been in race car pits watching the mechanics perform what can only be called magic, given the speed at which they work. I go to so many different places and meet so many different people that I would never be able to otherwise.

I work with writers and artists and directors, quite an entertaining crowd all by themselves. Having them depend on me for their raw material, if you look at the talent that way, is a thrill. It's always a new problem of how to find the right people for a new project.

Like almost any professional, I would be nothing without my support staff. My husband is my partner and he takes care of the video production and the finances. I could never do any of that! Also, if I'm casting for a commercial, the local colleges and universities loan me theater kids to help out. I love working with them. I'm their teacher for these few days, but the real world is our laboratory. Their energy is contagious. It's fun to get them up to speed, get them to see that this profession is something you can actually make a living at.

How many parents do you know who would encourage their kids to go into this line of work? "There's no security in that," they'll say. Which I find ironic, because chances are it's coming from someone who's just been laid off from a job in manufacturing management. Job security is passé. Get over it. I think people who are educated in theater are particularly employable. Why? Because they work to task. They work in teams. They put together projects quickly and meet deadlines.

Now I teach acting in The Theatre School at DePaul University, one of the best in the world. I'm thrilled to be there. As an acting teacher, I love to go to my students for help. They're smart, they're willing to work long hours, and they're fun to have around. They also make me a better teacher. I've been teaching for almost thirty-five years and it's my first love. I've been casting about half that long. I do it mostly on weekends to make money for the summer.

I get asked for career advice all the time. And I shrug. I always knew what I wanted to do. I wanted theater to be my life, though I didn't always know how that would play out. I think if you have a gift for something, you know early on. I did. The biggest hurdle young people face is trusting their instincts about what they love and what they're good at. They listen too hard, sometimes, to what other people have in mind for them. I agree with Joseph Campbell, who said, "Follow your bliss."

I think casting holds the secret to career choice. Just because it's a snap judgment doesn't mean it isn't right on. Don't overthink your life. Ask yourself, "What is the most fun you could have?" Give yourself a few seconds to answer. Then do that.

Dr. Michal Barszap

TRAVELIN' MAN

I was a professor at Ohio State University and taught Russian. I took my students to Russia in 1975 when nobody was doing that. At the time, there was this image of Red Russians who would attack you on every corner, which I knew was a farce. But you might be surprised by how many people told me, "You are out of your mind." Everyone said that. Everyone except the students. They came back and raved about the trip. They loved the experience.

The way I looked at it, I was a professor. I didn't care so much about the politics. I wanted these young adults to know that Russians—whom many people in this country considered the enemy in the mid-1970s—are people just like us. People are people. We can be friends. I wanted my students to meet students in that country, visit them in their homes, have fun with them. I grew up in Poland and was sixteen when we moved to the United States. The idea of getting along with people no matter where they live did not seem radical to me.

I went on to teach at Denison University and Texas A&M University and continued taking my students on these trips. Word got around and the trips became more popular, and soon we were traveling all over Europe. Hundreds of nonstudents asked me to put tours together for them, too. Eventually it got to be too much, arranging tours *and* being a professor. These were two full-time jobs and, while I loved teaching, I felt like I could make a bigger difference by developing awareness of other areas of the world. So I decided to concentrate on the tours.

Some of the people who discouraged me from this dream were travel agents. I found that ironic. They had all kinds of problems setting up trips to places I was now routinely taking my clients. I think the biggest reason I had an easier time doing it was because I expected to have an easy time. If you concentrate on problems, you will perpetuate them. Concentrate on solutions. That's what I did, and it literally opened a new world for me.

I work in the travel business full-time now. I'm a tour operator, I put together packages, and I couldn't be happier. If you go on one of my tours, you will do a lot more than just look at things. You are going to experience the culture you're visiting. That's the emphasis.

A lot of people wonder if the work they're doing matters to people. I don't have to wonder, because my clients are great about telling me how much my tours have meant to them. They get home after one of our trips and they don't forget about us. They call, they write letters, they seem intent on making sure I know how much they appreciate everything. "Thank you very much," they'll say. "That was the experience of my life." It makes getting up in the morning and starting all over again a joy.

People sometimes tell me I have a dream life because what they do on vacation—travel—I do constantly. Vacationing is my business. And while it is a dream life, it's also a job. But I wouldn't trade places with anyone who has a so-called normal way of making a living. This was my dream and I went for it. What strikes me is the number of people who told me I was a total idiot for doing that.

The best thing I ever did for myself was smile politely and say "thank you" before ignoring the naysayers. Now the same people who criticized me say I "was in the right place at the right time." Isn't that funny? But I always knew that if you have a dream, it is your *job* to make that dream come true.

Taimi Gorman

DOG MOM

You want help with marketing and publicity? You've come to the right place. No gibberish. No bull. And you'll get your money's worth—guaranteed. That's because I've run many successful businesses and I know what it takes.

The Doggie Diner in Bellingham, Washington, was—if you'll forgive me—a pet project. I'd just become a new dog mom and was sneaking my "child" everywhere. There weren't any places where you could go and be inside somewhere with your dog. There were outdoor cafés that would let you have your dog beside you, sure, but it rains a lot in this area—so I got it in my head to open a restaurant that would cater to dog owners.

I'd been in the restaurant business a long time by then and knew it was going to take quite a sales pitch to convince the health department to go along. The Doggie Diner was going to be next door to my other restaurant. "I want to serve people food at this diner," I said. "How do we do that?" We came up with the idea to serve the people food as a "to go" order from our other restaurant. That was the answer. You'd pick up the people food as takeout and bring it next door to this restaurant, where you could linger with your dog. The Doggie Diner wasn't even legally considered a restaurant—it was classified as a retail store.

But you might not have wanted to tell the dogs that.

We told people if their dog was missing to check our place first. If the dogs got out of the house, they were right down there. They'd just get up on a bar stool and order something. We sold peanut butter pups, garlic cheese chews, and mutt muffins. People drove hundreds of miles just to see the place, and it was fun to work there.

Though once in a while it was heartbreaking. I'll never forget the party who brought in a dog that was dying of cancer. They were putting him to sleep the next day and they brought him there for his last meal. They sat at the bar and the dog got whatever he wanted to eat. Everybody had a real good time, except for the staff—who kind of huddled in the back room, crying.

The Doggie Diner was an idea that worked. Not every idea I've had has worked, of course. But you have to be willing to take the risk. A lot of people spot opportunities. "Wouldn't this be fun?" they'll say . . . and leave it at that. At some point, you have to be willing to jump off the cliff and go do it.

It may not work. I've had some miserable failures. But you have to give yourself a chance. Keep saying yes. To yourself, to your dreams, to the possibility you'll fail— and the chance to start right over again.

Helen Gurley Brown

HAVING IT ALL

I didn't realize life was precious as much as I knew the things I hoped to have someday. The most important one being, maybe, some kind of security—both financial and emotional. For a long, long time my hard work had to do with having an invalid sister to support. She had polio before the Salk vaccine and she was in a wheelchair. My mother was a very sad and depressed person because her husband, my father, was squashed in an elevator accident. He ran for the elevator and made it, but the door crushed him. In those days, in Little Rock, Arkansas, elevators didn't have safety devices.

So I had to hit the deck running when I was eighteen years old. The minute I got out of high school, my family needed me to make a living. And all those years, pretty much every day, I just got up and did the best I could. Not because I was inspired, but because I had to. Later in life, after you've done that for quite a while, you find out that good comes from dedication. And you don't even have to aim that high. I had seventeen secretarial jobs before I finally was encouraged to write advertising copy at one of the agencies where I worked. My point is that you just get up every day and do the best you can. In my case, there was no way I could not do that because I didn't want my mother, my sister, and me to starve to death. It wasn't inspiration as much as necessity.

After you've done the best you can for a while, the rewards start to pour in. In my case, it didn't happen until I was in my thirties. I got to be very successful at copywriting. When I was forty, I had a chance to write my book *Sex and the Single Girl.* It was a huge success, but it didn't come about because I said, oh boy, I'm going to write a big best seller. It came about because it was the next thing to do. The opportunity was there so I did it. And after that came *Cosmopolitan,* and it was the same thing. I didn't know what I was doing when I started the new edition of *Cosmo.* I just went down to the office and tried to figure out how to be a magazine editor, because I had never been one before. The first day on the job, that night, after dinner—it was very late—my husband, David, was looking for me. He couldn't find me. He thought I'd gone to bed but I hadn't. Eventually he found me curled up under his desk in a fetal position. I was just absolutely terrified because I'd never been in a magazine office before, let alone the boss of a whole bunch of people.

But I was starting to find my place in the world. I don't think you have to figure it out immediately. If you keep trying things and scooching around, you'll discover an area that works for you. I don't know that anybody is sure, when they're sixteen or eighteen or nineteen years old, what they want to do. If it takes a while to find out what your calling is, that's okay. There *is* something you can do better than others, though. Let's find out what it is.

It's a lovely feeling when you find it, and it's gone on like that forever for me—the feeling that this is what I was born to do. It was wildly gratifying to edit the U.S. edition of *Cosmo.* For thirty-two years, *Cosmo* was a tremendously successful magazine, selling in the top ten at newsstands almost the entire time. That came to an end for me, to be the perpetrator of all that success, when a new editor came in and took my place. It was the right thing to do, so I have a different life now. But I'm working for really enlightened management. They are kind, generous, and grateful. Grateful for what I gave them all those years on the cheap, as it were. And they decided I'd go out the window or up the walls or into the river if I didn't have a job, so they gave me one.

I'm editor of *Cosmopolitan* International, of which there are now, oh Lord, fifty-seven editions. And in my first two years in this job, we kept opening up new editions. There were about twenty when I came in, but then we added thirty-seven new ones.

On a typical day the editions of the magazine from all over the world come across my desk. I go over them with my little yellow sticky notes, and I comment on virtually every page. I can't read each magazine in its own language, but the international editors can all speak English, so they can read my memos. I can tell from the pictures, though, what they're doing right and what they're doing wrong. There is a *Cosmo* format. It works all over the world. You are not put into this job to create your own magazine, to reinvent the wheel. And yes, you must take care of cultural differences. Things are a little different for women in Portugal than they are in Korea or in Johannesburg, but there is a basic *Cosmo* formula, and you don't change that any more than you change the formula for Coca-Cola or McDonald's or Levi's. This is what you do.

A lot of people have thought about retirement by the time they're my age, but I love that I can still contribute to the world. My husband, who's ninety-two, still produces movies. We'll go on a QE2 cruise and give lectures—he on movies and me on magazines—and draw big crowds. David says we're absurd. We should have retired years ago, but we didn't. We missed the boat, and now it's too late. We're too old!

My legacy will be my books, my legacy will be *Cosmopolitan*, and maybe my legacy will be—if anyone remembers—that I said, "Get out there and do it. There's something you can do; let's find out what it is." It doesn't have to be big stuff. You don't have to be a famous model, or a writer, or a television star. You don't have to be a Nobel laureate. Just find something you can do. Whether it's cooking or gardening or taking care of children, get to be real good at it. I'll keep you encouraged. That legacy—of helping women find themselves and do their best—that could be on my tombstone.

Marshall Goldsmith

GOOD COMPANY

I'm an executive coach. I help really successful people—
CEOs at many of the world's largest corporations—become even more successful. That's the subject of my most
recent book, *What Got You Here Won't Get You There.*
The most important thing I teach is, identify the behavior
that's annoying people—and stop it. Although what I offer
is very simple and easy to understand, it is hard to do!

I got into this work when I was a college professor. I met
a famous man, Paul Hersey, a pioneer in the field of leadership development. I learned about him, I got to meet
him, and he was kind enough to invite me to programs
that he did. I went to a lot of those with him. He got
double booked one day and he said, "Do you think you
can do what I do?" I said, "I don't know." He said, "I'll
pay you $1,000 for one day." I was making $15,000 a year
at the time. So I said, "Well, sign me up." I went to work
with him and got good at it. That's how I got into the
business, and I've been doing it now for thirty years.

An exercise I've been doing lately involves four elements of conversation. "Tell me," I say, "how much time in your organization is spent on the following: talking about how wonderful you are, listening to someone talk about how wonderful he or she is, talking about how bad or inept someone else is, or listening to someone talk about how bad or inept someone else is?" The answer—from more than a thousand people I've polled—is, "More than 50 percent." I think a great productivity-enhancing strategy is reducing those conversations.

I travel a lot, and I overhear a lot. It strikes me how often we remind people we're talking with—even those we don't know very well—how intelligent we are. It's human nature, but it's not an attractive part of that nature. It's difficult for smart, successful people to hear someone tell us something we already know and not point out that we already know it. It's much better to say, "Gee, that's interesting. Thanks." There's no harm in just saying thank you.

This is particularly important if you're the boss. I teach a concept called feedforward. You ask for ideas and when you get them you say, "Thank you." That's it. Thank you. If it works for you, use the idea. If it doesn't work for you, don't use it. But look at it as a gift. When someone gives you a gift, you don't say, "Stinky gift. Bad gift. Stupid gift." No. You just say thanks. If you don't want to use the gift, put it in the closet. Don't insult the person who gave it to you. If you're managing people and you ask for feedback and then argue with it, good luck getting anyone to be honest with you ever again. It's almost a disease, I think. I call it "adding too much value."

I have an undergraduate degree in math and I'm big on measurement. It's my conviction you can measure soft skills, and that's an essential part of my teaching and coaching. Let's take listening. If you were my client and you told me you wanted to become a better listener, I'd say, "As judged by whom?" Your answer might be, "As judged by the following ten people." Then you get in the habit of asking those people for input. You say, "I want to be a great listener. Give me some ideas for how I can demonstrate that in the next month." You follow up with those people on a regular basis. You actually use a scale that says, "How much more effective have I become at listening?" The scores are all the way from minus five, which is less effective . . . to zero, no change . . . to plus five, much more effective. There's your result. Have you become better at the behavior you picked as judged by the people you picked?

I hold myself to the same standards, by the way. I get paid on results, as opposed to time spent with a client. If my clients improve, I get paid. I wrote a magazine article called "It's Not About the Coach." The client I spent the least amount of time with was the client who improved the most. He taught me a great lesson. He said my whole job is selecting the right clients. The way my coaching process works depends on choosing clients who are serious, who are dedicated. If I work with people who are dedicated and take this process seriously, they work hard and they get better. If I work with people who don't care, it's a complete waste of my time. So I only work with people who care.

I love my work. It's a combination of three things, really: teaching, coaching, and writing. Teaching is what I love the most. The coaching part is where I learn the most. And writing helps me have the biggest impact.

I think anyone can change. It's the old "gun to your head" test. If someone held a gun to your head, could you focus in and be a good listener? Yes? Then you can be a good listener without the gun! It's a question of priorities. A lot of excuses people give for not being able to change are just that—excuses. I think most of it is a crock.

Some leaders think that because they're successful, everything about them must be okay. It's superstition. "I behave this way, I am successful, therefore I must be successful because I behave this way." They don't ask if they're successful because of their behavior, or in spite of it. People are successful because they do many things right in spite of doing some things that are stupid. I've never met anyone so wonderful they had nothing on that "in spite of" list.

Peter Drucker said the leaders of the past knew how to tell, while the leaders of the future know how to ask. Most of us, today, manage knowledge workers who know more about what they're doing than their boss does. If you're managing people who know more about what they're doing than you do, it's kind of hard to tell them what to do and how to do it. You have to ask, you have to listen, and you have to learn.

At the end of my classes, people sometimes ask each other if they plan to do what I've taught them. Almost all of them say yes. If I go back a year later, I'll find about 30 percent of the class hasn't done what I've taught. It isn't because they're bad people. It isn't because they don't want to change. It's because they're stuck in the same daydream I bet you've had. "I'm incredibly busy right now," they say. "There's a lot of pressure at work and at home, with new technology that follows me every-where, and with global competition. I feel about as busy as I ever have. Sometimes I feel out of control. I don't admit it to others, but I'm often overcommitted. But you know, I'm working on some very unique and special chal-lenges right now, and I think the worst of this is going to be over in four or five months. After that, I'll take two or three weeks and get organized. I'll spend some time with the family and start my healthy life program. After that, everything will be different and it won't be crazy anymore."

What I've learned is that tomorrow is likely to be just as crazy as today. Two or three weeks from now, it will be the same. Ask yourself what you're willing to change now, and change it. Don't wait for someday. If you have a dream, go after it now. If you don't work up the nerve at twenty-five or thirty-five, it isn't necessarily going to get easier when you're forty or fifty years old. And that's the kind of thing you'll regret on your deathbed. It's the same with your family and friends. Make time for them now. Have fun now.

Let's take what many people consider their most important job, parenting. I've asked thousands of parents to complete this sentence: "When my children grow up, I want them to be _____." No matter what country I'm in, there's one word that comes up more than every other word combined. You've guessed it. The word is *happy*. People say, "I want my children to be happy."

So this is my advice: You want your children to be happy? You go first. Let them watch you be happy.

SEVEN

Have Fun!

People keep asking me, "What do you want to be when you grow up?"

Man, the pressure to find a good career starts early.

So when I'm surfing the Internet, I go to *The Career Clinic* website.

I get daily career advice . . . and links to other career-related sites, too.

Then I go to Barney Online, 'cause I'm not ready to grow up that fast.

—Katie Anderson, *The Career Clinic*

There's only one problem with that little jingle, recorded by my daughter when she was five. It wasn't true. "That's what you do in advertising," I teased her. "You lie." That remark made her very unhappy. She's a stickler for the truth. So I changed the subject. "What *do* you want to be when you grow up?" I asked. "I don't know," she said. She fumbled around. At first it was a glassblower. Then a singer. No! A professional tennis player. She paused. "I know!" she said. "A clothing designer." More thought. Another pause. And then, "I'm not ready to decide. When it's time to pick a job, I'll just do whatever sounds like the most fun."

My stickler for the truth, I thought, stumbled on the only truth that's been a reliable compass for me. Have fun. That's it.

I love my work, but I really love being a mom. I thought I was setting a great example for Katie. Marshall Goldsmith knew I could do better.

Marshall is the executive coach you met in the last chapter. Katie came with me to a conference where we shared a table with Marshall at lunch. He had a question for me about guilt. "I am 100 percent motivated by guilt," I blurted out, too surprised by the question to answer it more . . . slowly.

"Is that the example you want to give Katie?" he asked. "Do you want her to feel guilty when she's doing nothing wrong? Do you want her to knock herself out, then beat herself up for not doing more?" Of course not. "Well, then . . ." The room got very quiet as I reached for a Kleenex. "Don't worry," Marshall said. "Everyone cries when I do this."

"Let me ask you something," he said, not letting up. "Pretend you're ninety-five years old. What advice would that woman have for you?" I thought about it. "Give yourself credit for what you're pulling off," I finally said. "So do that," he suggested. "Now. And often."

Katie and I marked this lesson when we got home. "What do you think it means?" I asked her. "It means," she said with confidence, "when I want to play on the computer, you can go do your own thing and not worry about me. It was *my idea*." We grinned at each other.

Katie was old enough to appreciate what a thrill it was for me to get a literary agent. I called her at school the day it happened. "Mommy!" she practically screamed later, when she dropped her backpack on the playground and raced toward me for a hug. Maybe she knew what a gift I'd given her, by going after my own dreams. She won't feel guilty for growing up and leaving a giant hole in my life. She'll leave a giant hole all right, but she knows I'll go back to more of what I loved doing before "mom" got added to my resume.

In the meantime, I do my best to set a good example. I tell her the truth, and we have fun.

Rex Walker

COWBOY

My life is straight out of *City Slickers.*

I could have done anything I wanted. I graduated from the University of Colorado with a degree in petroleum geology and worked for Mobil Oil, but all I ever wanted to be was a cowboy. Instead of fighting that, I gave in. I gave in early, and I have never looked back.

I first got the itch at eleven, working on a dude ranch. I became friends with the owner and spent summers in Colorado working for him. I've been working with horses ever since.

Now I own Sombrero Ranches, which is based in Boulder. Our principal business is made up of tourists who come to Colorado, Wyoming, and Arizona. We have the concession in the Rocky Mountain National Park, where we furnish horses on guided tours from two hours to all day. I also own businesses in Mexico, where I rent homes to American tourists. Not many people want to ride horses in the snow in Colorado, so I spend my winters in Mexico.

On the ranch, we usually start our days about seven o'clock with a breakfast ride. We take people out and ride them way back up in the hills for an hour and fifteen minutes. Once we get up there, we feed them sausage and eggs and pancakes, all they can eat—then bring them back. That's how I start each morning. On the ride I can get my thoughts together for the rest of the day, which is inevitably very hectic but also very enjoyable. People continue to come and ride throughout the day, and occasionally I'll go on some of those as well, but usually there are a lot of other things that come up that need my attention.

We're the largest horse company in the world. We have 1,800 head and employ 150 people on different ranches around the country. My whole family is involved, my kids, their spouses, everybody. It takes every one of us a lot of time to make it work right because we really want it to be a good experience when someone comes and rents a horse.

I love to see the transformation in people when they learn there's more entertainment out there than the latest Nintendo game. It's funny. Some people ride for an hour and think they're going to die because they're so stiff and sore afterward. Most people in this country have never ridden a horse. They don't realize how many muscles you use. They say the outside of a horse is good for the inside of a man.

It's certainly been good for me. Fifty years into it, I can't imagine another life.

Regrets? You have to be kidding.

Dave Barry

TAKING MY HUMOR SERIOUSLY

I didn't really think about what I wanted to be when I grew up. I was not a career-oriented kid. I was the class clown, sure, but there were a lot of class clowns. And I always used humor in my relationships with my classmates and my family. I just didn't set out to be a humor writer. I liked to write, and if you had asked me to describe the ideal job, it probably would have been this one. But I didn't think a job like this actually existed and so I really didn't orient myself that way.

I started out working for newspapers. After that I taught effective-writing seminars. I kept writing columns, though, and the columns caught on. Enough papers ran them that eventually the *Miami Herald* offered me a job, and that's how it all happened.

When I got to the *Herald*, I thought, oh, this is cool, I can actually do this for a living. I know it's what I'm happiest doing, and I can't imagine having a job where I had to do something actually useful or productive—like go to a real office and build things, or anything like that.

I don't have any trouble finding material. That's what writing is. It's not really writing as much as thinking about what it is you're trying to say. But I'm used to that. It's what I've done for so long now. Although I periodically announce that I can't do it anymore because I suck at it.

Does it feel like I'm always at work, in that everything is fodder? No. I don't think that way. I really don't. I probably would if I had to write more often. But if anything, I have too many things to write about, so it's not like I'm going around desperately thinking, gee, I have to have a funny experience now. To the extent that happens, it's likely to be that something bad happens. Like my car breaks down or my computer doesn't work. And at the time, the last thing I'm thinking is, this is funny. I'm thinking, Jesus, my computer broke. It's only later, when I've dealt with it, that I'll think, oh, maybe I can write about that. But I almost never say to myself, in my day-to-day life, "Oh, fodder."

I would just as soon not, in fact. I don't think you would be really living if you were going around viewing it as fodder. I have read columnists who seem to make everything that happens to them like a sitcom, and I don't believe them. I know they're going to a lot of effort to make life funnier than it actually is. It rings kind of dishonestly to me when I see somebody writing, every week, about his or her kids or his or her life. I think, no, your life really isn't that funny. Come on. You're lying.

And just in case you're thinking about *Dave's World*, that TV show supposedly based on my life, they ran out of plots that came from my columns pretty quickly. I watched it maybe half the time, but it was a little bit creepy for me to have a guy with my name having these wacky experiences I never had.

I love what I do. The work is the same. It's always hard and it's always scary and it's intimidating. But it's also always thrilling when you finish. It's a very satisfying thing to create something and send it out.

I love writing, but I have no illusions about the significance of my work. This is not false modesty. It's really easy to overemphasize the importance of what I do. The easiest way for me to remind myself is to think of my hero, Robert Benchley. He was a great humor essayist in the first half of the twentieth century, and I love his work. He isn't alive anymore, but he was terrific in his time. But if you say his name to an audience today, the sixty-year-olds and up will nod their heads, and nobody else will have a clue who he is. I make people laugh, and that's a good thing to do. It's much the same as what the comics do, what *Dilbert* does. But as far as long-term significance, I don't think there is much.

I am proud, though, that I have been reliable and consistent for a long time—which is to say, I took my humor seriously. I produced it regularly and kept it fairly consistent so that if you liked it, you'd keep liking it. Although fans come and go. But generally, I have been a fairly consistent humor writer for a bunch of years. It's more like pride in craft than anything. And again, this will sound like false modesty but it's real modesty: I don't think of myself as being, in any way, on a par with really good writers, literary writers. I think what I do is difficult, and a lot of people who are great writers couldn't do it. But I don't confuse that with great literary skill or long-term social significance or anything like that. I don't even aspire to that, to be honest.

I think other writers who try to write humor know that what I do is difficult. And there are a lot of people who try and fail. Because it looks like it would be a great thing to be doing. Which it is. It's just that it's not as easy as it looks. And that's what I'm proud of. That I do something that's not easy, and I've done it for a long time. More than anything else, that's what I'm proud of.

As I get older, I'm more and more aware that time is finite. And I've become more sensitive, in recent years, to not giving all of my time to what I used to think of as being incredibly important. Like my career. It's not as important as my daughter or my son, my wife, my family. It's not as important as my friends. And now I find myself saying no to things that some people—or even I, twenty-five years ago—would have considered stark raving insane to say no to. It's just realizing that success is a means to an end, but it is not an end. The end is some kind of happiness and contentment.

Maybe when you're young, success by itself is enough. Oh wow, I'm making it. But I think if you still feel that way when you're my age, you're an idiot. You haven't learned anything. If you still think it's more important to be famous or rich or wildly popular with the public than it is to have good friends, or to be able to enjoy yourself just being alone, then you're not catching on. You're going to die unhappy. That's my guess.

There are so many things I love about my life. I have a wonderful family. I'm in a rock band of authors who are my friends. And the fact that I can do those things, that I have time for my family and time for my friends, I attribute to the fact that I've done okay at the profession I picked.

If you're looking for career advice from me, here's the cliché I'd go with: If you enjoy what you're doing, you'll be a lot happier. That goes without saying, I guess. But you're also more likely to succeed at it. Because you'll take it more seriously, you'll work harder at it, and you'll stick with it longer. I find that to be true. Although again, I didn't consciously live that way. I was doing other things that I didn't like as much, because I assumed that's what I had to do to stay alive. And there probably is some truth to that, because I wouldn't have been able to start right out as a humor writer. But as long as I kept writing humor when I could and kept that as part of my life, I kept the option open. It made all the difference. In the end that became my life.

My advice is, never forget what you want to do. I know a lot of people hear that message, but they don't do it. Especially kids. The generation of kids in college now, to judge from my son's friends, believes that they have to decide right away how to make a living, and right away take the right courses, and right away get on that career track or they'll fail. And I think that they'll be much less happy than if they risked a little more failure, had a little less security, early on, when you don't need it as much anyway, and experiment a little more with what they might really want to do.

Roxanne Ward

CALL OF THE WILD

I was raised on a farm and learned to hog call when I was about seven. I entered contests and always won. It seemed as natural as beauty pageants were for other girls. I was fascinated by little pigs. I watched my mom care for the piglets, and one of my favorite things to do was get down inside the pen and play with them. They talk to each other with their little grunting sounds and it's enchanting.

You cannot be in a bad mood when you're around pigs, and they were sort of a lifesaver for me. I had a very unhappy childhood. I can spare you the details—but there was no dancing through cornfields in my pretty sundress playing with lambies, let's put it that way. The pigs were another story. I could crawl around with them in the mud and feel right at home. The thing I loved best was how silly they looked when they were mad. They look like they're smiling even when they're angry, and I learned to do that as I grew up. It served me well.

People can't wait for me to hog call as soon as they find out what I do. Doesn't matter where. Doesn't matter when. How can I say no? Why would I want to?

I've hog called in church. "We have a special guest here," the minister will say before talking to the congregation about my . . . calling. I've hog called in the operating room before the doctors went to work. Though when the anesthesiologist had me do it before surgery it caused more commotion than usual, because people thought they'd started the operation without putting me to sleep. All of a sudden there was a swarm that descended on that little room with a chorus of, "Oh my God! Oh my God!"

In some ways I can relate to how pigs feel when they're on display at the state fair. Because radio stations will call me early in the morning for a hog call. Schools bring me in. Same with nursing homes. I take my two little pigs with me, Oscar Mayer and Petunia. Charles Gibson told me on *Good Morning America* that I have a God-given talent.

A lot of people think what I do for a living—and I do this for a living—is silly. Which is fine. I love to make people laugh. I love teaching people about pigs. You wouldn't believe how many kids have never seen a pig up close, and it's the greatest feeling in the world to see them discover what I love about the animal. It's a great way to teach children about farming. That's probably the best part of being a two-time world-champion hog caller: the doors it opens to the rest of the world. I get to meet people I never would have met otherwise, and make them laugh. That's my favorite thing right there. I never get tired of it.

Dave Holly

CLOWN

I found my mission in life in a nursing home in Ellsworth, Minnesota. I'd been hosting a radio talk show but was moonlighting as a clown. On this particular occasion, I entertained the residents with all the usual jokes and skits. I made the rounds, handing out clown stickers, and told each person they were magic. "Press his nose," I suggested. When they did, I squeezed a squeaker inside my glove. Most people figure it out right away, but they still enjoy the gag.

One resident wasn't amused. No matter what I did, she just sat there, expressionless. Finally I walked up to her and asked, "Would you mind if I gave you a sticker?" She shrugged. "Now this is a magic sticker," I told her. I pressed the clown's nose with one hand and squeezed the squeaker with my other hand. She looked down at the sticker, then back up at me. "Well, I'll be damned!" she said. I was on my way out of the building a little while later, waving good-bye, when I felt a tug on my arm. When I turned around, there she was. "Thank you," she told me, "for a wonderful day of entertainment."

That's why I'll never stop clowning. As to why I got started, I was just, uh, humoring my dad. Dad did some clowning a few times a year, and he invited me to a seminar about it. From the moment I put on grease paint I was hooked. I soon joined the Shriners in Sioux Falls, and after a few years with them I went into business for myself.

I work in radio, too, and get a lot of practice entertaining people. Ask anyone in radio why he got into it and chances are he'll tell you it was the chance to clown around for a living. I love radio. Your days start early, and you have an hour or two to figure out what to do for the rest of your shift. Every day you come in, you think you've heard the strangest, most bizarre thing that could possibly happen—and every day something trumps it.

My broadcasting career began as a teenager. I reported on Rock Rapids (Iowa) High School happenings for the radio station in nearby Luverne, Minnesota. That's where I got bitten by the radio bug you hear about. I kept stats during football and basketball games, and I suggest people who want a career like mine do the same. You have to give up the idea of starting out as a disc jockey. You have to be willing to get experience at whatever the station needs you to do. There are too many people competing for the same jobs for you to be very selective at first. Plus, the more things you volunteer at, the better you'll be able to decide what you'd like to get paid for doing.

It's only been fairly recently that clowning has added much to my personal bottom line. For a long time, it was hundreds of hours a year volunteering at community functions and charity events. I make some money doing birthday parties, but that's more a labor of love. My wife and I can't have children, so making kids laugh is especially thrilling.

The only thing I no longer love about clowning is twisting balloons. There are people who make a living doing only that. Even in a market the size of Sioux Falls, you can get a hundred dollars an hour. I'm happy to let others do it, though, while I focus on my keynote addresses. I start off as Dave and gradually transform into Deebo, the Hobo Clown. My message for businesspeople is simple but important. A lot of clowns are in it to look good. They spend two hours getting ready and might be as professional looking as you could find. But they forget that "clown" is also a verb. Your job is to make people happy. That's what I like to tell corporate types. You want to make sure you win the talent competition, not just the pretty pageant.

As to what my radio bosses think of my clowning, I've been lucky. It doesn't hurt my clowning business to be in the media, sure, but that's as likely to benefit my employers as it does me. Every time I make an appearance as Deebo, the radio station gets free publicity. Sioux Falls is a small enough community that I'm known for both roles. I don't think you can be appealing on the radio unless you reveal your personality, and clowning's a big part of who I am. Each job enhances the other. I love being in grease paint when someone walks up and says, "Hey, heard your radio show this morning." What I am and what I do are the same. I work seemingly around the clock, but it doesn't feel like work at all.

I can't imagine a better gig in life. I've been depressed at times, but when I look back I realize that what I learned from those experiences helped me get the life I have. So I have no regrets. I live by this motto: There's good judgment and there's bad judgment. Good judgment comes from experience. And experience? Well, that comes from bad judgment.

That's why I tell young people to forgive themselves for the times when they've been stupid. It's the secret to life.

I think each of us has God-given talents we'd best go with. They were given to you for a reason. Why fight it?

Anne Moore

PICTURE PERFECT

Seeing Oprah in one of my hats on the cover of her magazine was the best. It's my lifetime achievement award. It's been several years since it first happened, and I'll never get over the thrill.

I made my first hat when I was thirteen or so. I made a little dress out of a sheet, then trimmed it with ribbon. Then I found a hat in the marketplace and put a ribbon on that. I thought I was the grooviest thing in the world.

After I grew up I spent some time in Paris and worked at *Vogue.* I met all the designers and learned all the designer names. The exposure, I knew, would help me with my childhood dream of being a designer. Back in New York, I was just another young girl taking this job or that. I was an administrative assistant at Lancôme—nothing terribly creative, but great experience.

My first business, which I started in 1986, was hair bows. They were new then, and a friend at *Vogue* thought mine were beautiful. So I called the other magazines and took everyone a little basket filled with bows. It was as if this was my destiny, because every door opened to me and it seemed as if I was everywhere at the right time. Looking back it was magic. I worked hard, but it didn't feel like work. Suddenly there I was, the bow girl. Diana Ross bought one from my first press clipping ever, which fueled my excitement for years.

All the stores wanted my hair bows. The people at Bergdorf Goodman asked me to give a speech to introduce my spring collection—hair ornaments as big as hats. So I thought, why not? I asked if I could bring some hats over to the store as well. You could find hat bodies in the market in New York. You can just walk along the street and buy bases and then make your designs on them, and that's what I did, until I found a man who could make the shapes I wanted.

I sewed up eighteen beautiful hats for Bergdorf Goodman. They bought every single one and sold them out in two weeks. That's how I got into the hat business.

I was almost too successful at first, if you know what I mean. You have to stay calm as things take off, because a lot of people will want to invest in you and make your business huge—which may be okay, but maybe not right away. You have to stay focused on how you're going to get the orders to Neiman Marcus tomorrow.

I've learned to balance the plans other people have for me with what brings me joy—the work itself. My designs aren't complete until they frame a woman's face. You can have five different women try on the same hat, and on one of them it seems to come alive. You know it right away, and so does she. She feels beautiful, she's happy, and my work is done.

I have more celebrity clients than I could have ever imagined and my creations have been featured in major motion pictures.

I get asked for career advice sometimes, and it usually goes something like this: What you're meant to do with your life will probably come naturally. When I reflect on my childhood, it seems there was only one path for me— the one I found. I think people sometimes stray too far from what gave them joy as a child. Either that or they become so successful doing what comes naturally that now they're bogged down with the pressures of running a business. Investors are fond of telling you to go back to the reason you got into the business to begin with. Which in my case is designing. It's seeing the look on a woman's face that tells me she feels as beautiful as I did at thirteen, when I realized I had a knack for design. That to me is the definition of fun.

Vicki Jo Ferriss

ART FROM THE FARM

Gardens are beautiful all by themselves, but I have a perennial garden and I'm perennially looking to improve on it. One day I noticed a roll of barbed wire—which we have plenty of—but for some reason it jumped out at me. "That's it!" I thought. "I can make something interesting out of *that.*" I started with a basket and everyone liked it. So I made more baskets, and then I made angels and flowers.

At one time, I would have called myself a frustrated artist. I tried making little crafty things, but they never took. I did some stained glass, but it just wasn't my thing. Maybe it wasn't challenging enough. It takes a lot of strength to sculpt barbed wire, and there's always the risk of getting poked. I wear heavy leather gloves, but sometimes they're no match for the medium if you hit it just right. So it's hard work. As a farmer, I'm no stranger to that.

We have your typical fourth-generation Iowa farm, if there is such a thing. Corn, soybeans, hay, oats. It's a tough living.

My artwork helps to even out our income somewhat. Not only that, but I'm winning awards and becoming known for this medium. It's very unusual. I think that's a big reason it's becoming so popular. Anyone can hang a mirror or a painting over his or her fireplace. A wall hanging made of barbed wire is more of a conversation starter.

I don't make patterns. I'm not one to measure anything. I'm not a precise person. I'm a very casual person. That's one of the things I enjoy most about the work. I can do it any way I want. I love designing pieces—which include custom signs in addition to wall hangings and sculptures—and I love seeing how they turn out. It's always somewhat of a surprise. Most of all, I love sharing my creations with people, whether they live nearby or I meet them at a craft show or farmers' market.

Another thing I love about the work is how many happy memories it evokes. It brings back a simpler time for some of my clients, maybe when they were growing up on a farm themselves. You might have heard of people who buy tractors just for their sentimental value. I can relate.

Most people don't look at barbed wire and think, wow, how beautiful. To me it's just another raw material, something that—with hard work and creativity—will nourish your spirit.

Jeffrey Zachmann

KINETIC SCULPTOR

I play with marbles for a living. I am not kidding. I make kinetic sculptures, or what some people call marble runs. They're basically stainless steel frames with tracks for marbles. An electric motor takes them to the top and gravity brings them back down again, almost like in a fountain. My booth is always among the most popular at art festivals. I used to be a potter, and back then, if I was really busy, I'd have four or five people in my booth at once. Now there are thirty or forty people crowding around.

The marble runs are often mistaken for perpetual motion. A lot of people ask me how to shut my sculptures off. I show them the cord and the switch, and it's only then they realize the pieces don't run by themselves. You can get so absorbed watching the marbles roll down the tracks you don't notice the motor at the bottom.

Making a living as a potter was a feat in itself. I did that for about fifteen years. I was doing the marble runs on the side and realized they were more fun. So I switched. I had studied art at what's now Minnesota State University in Moorhead. My ceramics instructor gave us an assignment that changed my life: "Make something nonfunctional out of clay." I thought back to when I was a kid. There was a big pile of dirt by my house and I'd go out with my friends to make trails and tunnels on little hills. We put marbles on them and watched them make their way down. I tried to replicate that experience in college with clay, and it worked marginally well.

Clay has a lot of limitations. It shrinks and warps as it dries. You have no idea how the balls will run after it's fired. So I'd make one piece and that might work, but the next ten wouldn't. After I left college and became a potter, I kept monkeying with the clay, trying to make it work with marbles. Then one day it hit me. Just because I'm a potter doesn't mean I can *only* work in clay.

I started working in metal. I already knew how to weld from building equipment for my pottery, and was surprised by how well metal worked. Suddenly I had a whole new product line, kinetic sculptures, and it was exciting.

Exciting and scary. The thought of showing the sculptures to anyone did not enchant. They were unlike anything I'd ever seen, and I was afraid people wouldn't like them. I didn't want to take them to shows. Would you put your newborn up on a stand for strangers to gawk at? Would you ask them, "Do you think this is a cute baby?" Probably not. What if they didn't like what they saw?

My wife finally talked me into doing some shows. The kinetic sculptures were a hit. And I said, "Okay. I'm going to give myself six years to make this work." I knew building a clientele would take time and I wanted to give the medium a chance. Why six years? I didn't want to fail for not having tried long enough.

The first year I did three shows. I don't know if the first one counted because it was just a little one here in Fergus Falls, Minnesota, where I live—and I was the cochair. The next one was also small, a fiber/metal show in Minneapolis. The third one I got into was the Smithsonian Craft Show in Washington, D.C., a huge deal. Within six months, I didn't have time to do pottery anymore. It took off that quickly. It's been difficult, ever since, to keep up with orders.

It's also difficult to estimate what a typical piece is. The sculptures I have in my booth at art shows start at about $2,500 each. An average sale is between $4,000 and $5,000, and I was recently asked to do a proposal for a sculpture that would cost more than $300,000.

That's a lot of money to pay for something you just sit and watch. Though it's surprising how many people don't hesitate. It's a select clientele I have. And I joke with people that I can't afford my own work. That's what many artists find, that they can't afford to buy what they've created. I've had to raise my prices as I've gone along because otherwise I'd never be able to keep up with the demand.

When I started working in metal, I decided that every sculpture would be one of a kind. I like making them more than anything. I like going to shows and watching people fall in love with them too, but what I'm really in it for is the tinkering. When I was a potter, I'd design one cup and made that same cup for ten years because it represented part of a set. People wanted that repetition. After a while it kind of sucks the artistic soul right out of you. But with kinetic sculptures, the thrill is having something in your home—or your office building—you know nobody else has. So every time I go into my studio it's to make something no one has ever seen before. I don't get bored. People ask, "What's your favorite sculpture?" I always tell them, "The next one."

I'm living a dream. If you asked your friends, "Is it possible to make a great living playing with marbles?" they'd probably look at you like you'd lost yours. People want to know what made me think I could succeed doing this kind of work. All I can say is, I *didn't* think I could do it. That's been part of the fun. I'm as surprised as anyone else. A lot of the visitors to my booth want to know what my real job is. "I don't have one!" I say. "This is it!" I don't blame them for being jealous. Not that they would have necessarily traded places with me in the early years, of course. Almost every life looks good once you figure out how to make a living at your passion. It's the uncertainty people pass on, and you can't have one without the other. It's the old high risk, high reward.

If you want to talk about twists and turns, the learning curve on this career has been a good example. My mom was the creative one in our family and my dad was a mechanic. I pulled from both of those paths. Pottery taught me a lot about managing risks and running my own business. If I had begun my artistic career making kinetic sculptures, I probably would have failed because I wouldn't have known how to market my work. And even with the pottery, I eased into it. I did part-time work on the side to even out the financial ups and downs.

You may be surprised how many artists make a very good living having the times of their lives, though I would have done this work for a lot less than what I'm making. I've been at it for a long time and I still have this urge to pinch myself. I'll be playing—I mean working—on the latest sculpture and have to remind myself *this* is my *job*.

It's so much fun that people always want to know what I plan to do when I retire. I want to ask them, "Retire from what? Having fun? No thanks."

Roger Welsch

PREACHER

I don't know if you remember the *CBS News Sunday Morning* segment "Postcards from Nebraska," but that was me. Those were my stories, and I'm here to tell you that contrary to what you might have heard, there is a whole lot about Nebraska worth writing home about.

I began spending a lot of time with the Omaha Indians in the early 1960s, and just fell totally in love with these people. To my great surprise, they were filled with information that mainstream America could use and had somehow ignored. Our pioneer forefathers were real idiots to ignore this stuff. They were eating crap. Often they had a taste of Indian food and loved it, but they didn't want to eat low-status food. I wanted to give it a try, so when I was up on the reservation with my friends, I started hauling home some plants. I wanted to grow them and learn how to cook them—medicine foods and so on.

So that's what I did. I grew milkweed and other wonderful things in my yard. One day I came home from vacation to find a yellow slip taped to my front door. My lawn had been condemned. The note said I had six days to remove all worthless vegetation.

I invited the weed inspector to come out. When he did, I asked him, "What's worthless here? What do you want me to remove?"

He didn't even know the names of these plants. So he said, "Well, what about that over there with the white flower?"

I said, "We ate that for lunch."

"Well, what about this yellow stuff over here?"

"That's supper."

I told him the only thing worthless was bluegrass. "Believe me," I told him, "I didn't do anything to encourage that crap." So we went around and around about my lawn. Then I did what, thank God, we can do in America: I ran for the weed board on a pro-weed ticket.

About that time, probably 1973, Charles Kuralt was coming through Nebraska and speaking to the Nebraska Press Association in Grand Island, close to where I live. He asked the people at his table, "Is there anything going on in Nebraska that might make a good 'On the Road' story?" This was back in the early days of that series.

And they said, "Yeah, there's this crackpot running for the weed board on a pro-weed ticket." So he called me, and I invited him over. We fixed up a huge weed salad and had a couple of bottles of wild grape wine. After that, every time he'd pass through the area, he'd stop by. I kept a file of stories for him, and we got to be friends. We got along very well.

Then in about 1986, he came to pick me up when I was giving a program at West Point, Nebraska. He was in the back of the room watching my gig. I played the banjo and talked about folklore and history and that kind of thing. And he said, you know, there are probably ten things you just said in that little speech that would be nice pieces for *Sunday Morning.* "How would you like to work for money instead of for free?" he asked. And I thought, well, hey, there's an idea.

So I got where I am by not mowing my lawn.

I was a teacher for many years, and in the beginning I taught at Dana College in Blair, Nebraska. Then Nebraska Wesleyan University and, after that, the University of Nebraska. To begin with I taught languages, German and French. But my love was always folklore, the traditions. The traditions of Germany and France, and then increasingly of the Plains and of America. And then, American folk humor. I like humor. I like to laugh. And so it was natural that I got interested in the tall tale. I started writing more and more along those lines. It's important to write for the academic community and for other scholars. But, because my interest is folklore, it's also important that I write for the people. The material comes from the people, and I wanted to speak to the people. I wanted to write for a popular audience, so the people I got the stories from in the first place would be able to read them and enjoy them.

I started writing a column for *Nebraska Farmer* called "The Liar's Corner," which led to a column in *Successful Farming*—which I still do.

My love of public speaking came as a surprise. As a graduate student in 1958, I was very shy. A nerd. And a terrible student. I was really miserable. But I had the incredible good fortune of living across the street from the chairman of the department—I was majoring in German. He knew my folks, and he gave me a teaching assistantship—pretty much out of pity, I think.

The moment I stepped in front of a class, I was home. I got to be the star, and I loved it. Right away I knew what people meant when they said the best way to learn is to teach, because I studied German like crazy after that. I didn't want to be humiliated in front of all those students. I got to be pretty good at German.

At the University of Nebraska, we had all of our classes anonymously evaluated by our students. One of them wrote, "Being in Welsch's class isn't like being in a class. It's like being in an audience." I didn't know if that was a compliment or an insult. I had a few students in my office at the time, so I asked them. One of them said something that really hit me hard. He said, "Actually, Rog, being in your class isn't like being in a class *or* an audience. It's like being in a congregation."

And I thought, man, that's it! I'm a preacher.

I had been too dumb to realize it, I guess. One of the things I've always said about the pioneers on the Plains is that they were not brave, courageous people. They were hopelessly stupid. They had absolutely no idea what they were doing, where they were going. They thought in two weeks they'd be in California when they'd barely gotten a start. I can identify with that.

Have you ever seen the movie *The Jerk*? That's me. Actually *The Jerk* is based on the story of Buddha. Buddha tried all of these different things—just like the Jerk did: success in business, becoming wealthy, living the aesthetic life, living a life of sex and drugs, all of it. And he eventually came back to the river, where he started. That was his story, and in many ways it's my story. The innocent bumbling through life, and being graced by God all the way. They say God takes care of fools and drunks.

I am very grateful for my life. I don't ask God for anything, because I think I have been so generously endowed over the years that I don't have anything more coming. I mostly just kind of hide and hope the gods don't notice me. We gave too much to this guy; maybe we ought to take a little bit out of his account.

I have been so lucky in my life and so fulfilled. Sure, there are things I'd still like to do, but I don't feel any panic that I haven't used my life well. I have a bookcase full of books that I've written. I have a wonderful wife, and wonderful children—all on amazing journeys of their own.

I've pretty much gone where my heart has led me and done some wacky things. I've solo-climbed mountains. I even went to Grand Prix racing school. That was after one day a few years ago, when I was lying on the couch moaning and groaning about how just once I'd like to drive a Formula race car. I said to my wife, "I'd give a thousand dollars to drive one of those cars around the track once in my life." So she found a school and said, "Go." Someone from one of the newspapers in Lincoln interviewed her and asked her what she thought about her husband, an older man with children, a professor, going off to drive race cars.

And she said, "Well, he's always wanted to be a race car driver and I've always wanted to be a rich widow. It all works out beautifully."

EIGHT

Try Something New When You Stop Having Fun

> You don't need endless time and perfect conditions. Do it now. Do it today. Do it for twenty minutes, and watch your heart start beating. You may not be able to stick with it that long! At the beginning you can only handle a little of that dream at a time. It's strong stuff.
>
> —Barbara Sher, *I Could Do Anything If I Only Knew What It Was*

I like to watch people at work. Are they happy? If they aren't, why don't they do something else? I'm struck by the seeming ease with which some people will leave a marriage. But a career? It's as if leaving a job is out of the question. And I think that's sad. You are allowed to change your mind.

I don't know what I want to be when I grow up, and I'm not all that interested in deciding. Trying to predict the future is not one of my hobbies. I'll take my story one page at a time, and hope it inspires.

Here's wishing *you* a great story.

Jan Parzybok

COLORADO POTTERY

I loved teaching. I gave it my whole heart for ten years. Then I got divorced. It wasn't my idea, and I suffered from it terribly. I had two young sons to think about, and the kids at school were getting the best of me—literally. I didn't have much energy left at the end of the day for my own children. With only so much "me" to go around, I thought, well, may as well turn the rest of my life upside down. I say it casually, but it was do or die. I wanted to be happy at my work. I wanted to be happy for my kids, and I wanted to be happy for me.

I ran into someone who was starting a pottery cooperative and asked if I wanted in. I'd always been interested in pottery. I studied it and collected books and went to workshops. Two roads appeared. I could run away or start drinking or do whatever else the freshly divorced set does to forget, or I could pour those feelings into clay. I had no experience running my own business or being a potter, which made it more appealing. If the upheaval consumed me, so much the better.

Here's what depressed me about teaching. You have great students in your class and you have poor students. You try to help them all, but you end up catering to mediocrity. The most depressing thing about that is how okay most parents are with it. They don't have high ideals for themselves, and the apple doesn't, well, you know . . . . The parents' attitudes upset me more than the administration. It was time to get out.

The minute I did, the more energy I had for my young sons. I raised them. We went on road trips. We went camping and fishing. We explored museums. Mostly we talked. And talked. And talked. You may have heard it said that kids don't remember what you said, they remember what you did. My kids remember the endless chats with Dad.

The thing is, the more I attended to my happiness, the happier we all were. They saw me struggle, of which I'm glad. I don't draw very well. I can't paint. I'm not very good at almost anything you'd consider artsy. I'm not even comfortable being called an artist. Maybe artisan or craftsperson. I'm a highly skilled technician.

I make pots quickly now, but every single one is a part of me. You can put it on the shelf in some store and someone either approves or disapproves. The ones who approve show their support with money, and that's how I got back into the world.

I suppose it shouldn't be a surprise I make my living this way. I used to skip classes in college to go to the pottery lab. My pottery professor was more of a painter than potter, and it wasn't long before he asked me to teach the class. You want to learn how to do something? Teach it. Those who can't do, teach. After a while, you learn.

One thing I pay attention to is how much anger I grew up with. It doesn't necessarily set me apart, but I've noticed what a settling effect clay has. A lot of potters seem to have a light approach to people, and I think the medium has something to do with it. I find my tensions go right off my shoulders, down my elbows, through my wrists, and into the clay. The clay will accept anything. That's a most satisfying aspect of potting.

It's tough to make a living, but it's a joyful way to live. The most fun is sitting behind the wheel throwing. You may think making fifty pots at one time would get old, but each is different and each is an expression of the clay and of me. That's one reason people like pottery. It's not something you pull down off of a shelf at Wal-Mart. It's part of someone's spirit.

Making a living by molding clay is like maintaining a good relationship. It's one of the most difficult things you'll ever do in life and it's one of the most satisfying. It's tough. You have to stay with it. You have to believe in yourself. The next time you're at a sales seminar, look around the room. There may be a few potters in there. We have to do the same things anyone else does to have a thriving business. You have to talk to people about their tastes; you have to go to arts and crafts shows and find out what's selling. Listen to other potters. Go to workshops. Yeah, network. Where's a good shop to sell pots?

Who's buying what? What shall we make? I spend a lot of time in the studio producing work, but you have to be everywhere else, it seems, all at once, getting that work out into the world.

I'm always amused by people who want to leave some corporate rat race to be a potter. The idea of running one's own studio is romantic. The reality is, it's a lot of work.

Not that I'm complaining. I have the same built-in aversion to sales that I think a lot of people do, but it's more of a nuisance than anything. The politics of teaching sucked the joy out of that work for me. The business of being a potter, while frustrating, shows me daily how much I want to be in that business. I can't *not* do this work. It's what I need to do to be happy.

So, when my younger son announced he wanted to be a potter, I told him, "No way." I discouraged him like crazy! There aren't many parents I know who greet news like this with, "Great! Let's go shop for a pottery wheel! Forget college. No problem." But those parents had nothing on me. I knew exactly why what he wanted to do was a bad move, and I fought it. We laugh about it now. My son eventually became a sculptor. He couldn't be happier, and I couldn't be prouder. Without knowing it, I became the test of how much he wanted the life of an artist.

I tell my kids to keep their minds open, keep their hearts open, and work like crazy. They roll their eyes at what I say, but take to heart what I do.

Michael Anderson

HOT DOG MAN

I sell hot dogs on a street corner in Alaska. From April through September, that is. I sell seven different varieties. One of them is reindeer. People are always surprised at that one—but it's an excellent hot dog.

I used to manage a health club. Before that I was in the restaurant business for more than fifteen years. I started out as a dishwasher and worked my way up. When I got into management I was thankful for having done the jobs I was managing. I don't think you can be effective otherwise.

I love being my own boss. I love doing my own thing and having control over everything. It's like running a small restaurant, except you have time to joke around with customers more. I get quite the cross section. We're talking judges, doctors, lawyers, cops, factory workers, stay-at-home moms, everyone you can imagine. I have a coffee shop downtown as well, but hot dogs are 98 percent of my income. I make enough in the spring and summer to spend a lot of the rest of the year traveling, and that's another thing I love about my life.

A lot of people tell me, "Oh man, you have it made." That used to get under my skin, because they didn't seem to realize how much effort went into getting to this place in my life. They didn't see the eighty-hour weeks in restaurant kitchens or the menial work I've spent years at. It looks like a dream job, and in many ways it is, but it hasn't been a dream life until fairly recently. It would be like aspiring to be an Olympic gold medalist without turning over eight hours a day of your life—for maybe decades—to train. But you can't have one without the other.

One day my mother told me the reason people latch on to me for advice on how to get a dream job is because I make it look easy. And I thought, "I can live with that." So here I am. This is my advice. It isn't easy, but it's possible, and it's worth everything you will go through.

I ask one thing from my work, besides a decent living. And that's happiness. A tall order? Yes and no. It seems like people feel guilty when they want a job that's fun. But with all the time most of us spend at work, I don't think you should feel guilty if you want to enjoy it. I think it's stupid *not* to want that. So when I'm not happy I move on. That's how I ended up here. I'd be in a restaurant, managing, and realize how stressful it had become. There was some drifting, going from job to job—though that experience paid off in a big way. I couldn't have this life without everything I've ever learned. It may sound goofy, but all my experience has led up to this—a hot dog stand. I couldn't be happier.

I don't scrimp. I don't compromise. And I don't cheat people. There. That's your recipe for success. I'm not going to cut back on products as the years go by just because I could. I'm going to give you more than I did the last time you stopped by, because I can.

I do company picnics, I do the state fair, and of late, I've also had some help, though not from people who claim to want to help. They show up with their growth schemes, telling me how I could do more of what I'm already doing. If you did this and this, they'll say, you could make a killing and you wouldn't have to sell hot dogs on the street.

No, *you* could do that, I feel like saying. I'm perfectly happy right here.

Bob Page

REPLACEMENTS

I was an auditor for the state of North Carolina and hated it. Nobody's glad to see you coming. I lived for Fridays and was depressed by Sunday evening, just thinking I had to go back to work.

I took refuge in my hobby: flea markets. I started buying and selling on consignment and running small ads—mostly for china and crystal. I kept information about clients on index cards I stuffed into a little three-by-five recipe box. I let people know what I found on my weekend travels, and one thing that struck me was how much demand there was for some of these older patterns.

It wasn't long before I had so much to do in the evenings and on weekends, answering the mail and returning phone calls, that I started plotting an escape from my life as a CPA. I thought I could make a living selling china and crystal. I didn't need someone else to run the numbers. And I must have done a pretty good job, because Replacements, Ltd. made a profit the first year.

It's been more than two decades, and now we employ about 550 people. There are a few employees who are out on the road buying product, but most of the merchandise is either brought in or shipped to us from the general public or a network of what we call Star Suppliers. We have about 700 of those suppliers nationwide who subscribe to an index detailing what we're trying to find for our customers. They take that information to flea markets, estate sales, and auctions. They find pieces we're looking for and ship them to us, and then we inspect the merchandise and mail them a check if we find the pieces acceptable.

We get patterns every day we've never had before, and that's always a thrill. Whatever you buy from us will be free of cracks or chips, guaranteed.

Replacements is known for customer service and helping people find something they never thought they would. We have millions of pieces in our facilities and give tours of our main building every thirty minutes. Rand McNally listed us as one of the top twenty-five free attractions in the United States. It's such a delight to see the look on customers' faces when they walk in. People often think they're going to a flea market and are shocked to see our showroom, which is 12,000 square feet and dazzling.

While much of our business is online, I still love to go out on the road buying. I don't know which is more fun, getting paid for work I love this much or solving problems for customers. You have young people who broke a wineglass while their parents were out of town and need a replacement shipped overnight. Celebrities who want you to replace a lid on a teapot. And media. *Animal Planet* did a story on us because we let our employees bring their pets to work. That was a policy I started after an employee gave me a dog for my birthday one year and I thought, I can't leave this dog at home. Now we probably have thirty or forty dogs in the building on any given day. In a china shop! But it works.

I don't even call it work anymore. I know so many people who are unhappy with their lives mostly because they hate their jobs. And you just want to shake them and say, "It doesn't have to be that way." I have a wonderful life, but it's because I took a risk. I didn't look at it that way at the time. I simply thought if it doesn't work out, I can always go back to being a CPA.

I think that's the one mistake people make when pondering a career change. They say to themselves, "What if it doesn't work out?" But they don't answer the question! What if it doesn't? You know what? You'll live.

I think the more important question is, "What if it *does* work out?" Maybe you can't handle that kind of happiness, having your dreams come true. I know plenty of people who make a career out of complaining and seem to enjoy it very much.

People often ask me for advice about starting their own business. The one thing I tell them is to make sure it's going to be something you love doing, because you'll be spending so much time at it. Life's too short.

Ben Garber

COMPUTER CONSULTANT

Greetings from Istanbul, Turkey. I work for the U.K. government, setting up centers all over the world to help people get a visa to come to the United Kingdom. It's part of the introduction of biometric finger scans and pictures to the visa application process. I'm training local staff for the contractor, Computer Sciences Corporation. I'm also doing some program design and management consulting. I've been to Egypt, Serbia, Algeria, and now Turkey. After this, who knows?

I had my own computer training and consulting business in the mid-eighties and most of the nineties. I was self-taught and loved the work. I loved the variety of clients—my time was divided between one-on-one coaching and classroom training. I also loved the work itself— meeting new people and teaching them how computers could help them get things done faster and better. I joked that I was the guy who actually read the books that came with the software and explained what they meant in plain English to my clients. It wasn't boring. It seemed like every twenty minutes the software versions changed and people had to be retrained.

I have a master's degree in social work and, as strange as it sounds, that's how I got into computers. Really. I worked with troubled young people and burned out on that after eight years. My last job in social work gave me some exposure to personal computers, which were quite a novelty at the time. I wanted to change careers and sold personal computers for a couple of years. Back then, that was a great way to get trained on them.

My next leap was to go into business for myself as a computer trainer. It was a risky move, in that my motivation was certainly tested. I worked out of my basement and had to treat walking downstairs the same way other people treat their morning commute—as a nonnegotiable part of being a grown-up—even though I didn't have a boss making sure I showed up.

So what gave me the courage? The better question is, "*Who* helped me find inside myself the courage I needed?" His name is Michael Bryant, and you may remember him from the second chapter. Michael's very much oriented toward the "do what you love," *What Color Is Your Parachute?* approach to career planning. He helped me see that if I wanted to start my own computer business badly enough, I could make it work, and he gave me the encouragement I needed until the dream became real.

Changing careers is like riding a bicycle. Once you learn how to do it you don't forget. The key words are *trans-*

ferable skills. People were always shocked when I told them I went from social work to computer consulting. "Oh, wow," they'd tell me, "that's completely different." And I'd tell them, "Well, yes, except that the things that helped me relate to people in social work were the same things that helped me relate to them when I was training them on computers."

By the midnineties, the world had changed and my business model didn't fit anymore. When I started my company few people had computers and a lot of them needed training. Suddenly it seemed like everyone had a computer. Even elementary school kids knew how to use them. So there wasn't quite the demand for someone like me. My experience with Michael Bryant helped me see that I'd reinvented myself once, and I could do it again.

That was in the back of my mind in early 2002, when I decided to become a professional speaker. My first wife, with whom I had started the computer business, had died from cancer in 1994, and a lot of what I spoke about in the beginning was bereavement and recovery. Then a friend who ran the Children's Theatre in Baltimore told me how much his funding had been cut and how he was going to do one-man shows instead of bigger productions. I had remarried in 2000 and my new wife, who has her own business doing leadership coaching and workshops, had just come back from a training program where she had seen a quote from Theodore Roosevelt about being "in the arena." Maybe you've heard it. It's about how the credit belongs not to the critic who stands on the sidelines but to the person whose face is covered by dust and sweat and blood, who's in the arena actually doing something. Not necessarily succeeding—but trying. I was very moved by that.

So I said to my friend, "What do you think about me doing character programs for kids as Teddy Roosevelt?" He loved the idea. I developed a presentation and took it not only to schools but eventually to corporations. I loved the corporate setting because what I offered wasn't the same old leadership seminar people had gotten used to. People saw me in costume and really paid attention. They saw that Roosevelt was an ordinary guy who did extraordinary things. He did many different jobs and never let himself be defeated by the circumstances of his life. I think I was drawn to portray him because I could relate to pressing on in the face of adversity and defeat.

I even made a sign inspired by Teddy Roosevelt to hang in my office. On one side it said, "In the Arena," and on the other, "Out of the Arena." It reminded me to define success in terms of effort and not just results. If I had a difficult call to make I turned the sign to read, "In the Arena." I gave myself credit for making the call and tried to detach from the outcome.

A funny thing happened on the way to becoming a professional public speaker. It didn't really work out. I loved speaking, but I only spent 10 percent of my time at it. The other 90 percent of my time was spent booking speeches. I know even dream jobs have aspects that aren't enjoyable, but this ratio was too lopsided for my taste. It was time to switch careers *again.*

I realized how much I missed training. I'm good at it. I was self-employed for more than twenty years and would have sworn I had no interest in working for someone else. I told myself that my training skills were limited to computer work. I thought I was too old to start over. Wrong, wrong, wrong.

I kept my sense of adventure, and that's how I found my way back to a career as a trainer. Believing in magic helped too. And by that I mean the magic of writing goals down before you set out to achieve them. As nuggets go, it's probably not the most original advice you've ever heard, but I'll tell you something. It works. I began to write down my goals to move my speaking work into training work. One of my action steps for those goals landed me the job I have now, doing training internationally. Write your goals down and keep them where you can see them. I keep a list of mine on my wall near my computer, and bring it with me when I travel.

Sometimes just writing a goal down is enough.

Quick story. After I remarried, my wife and I wrote a list of goals—both individually and as a couple. One thing I wanted was a canoe, and a month after I put that on my list, my brother called. He said, "I saw a canoe in the newspaper. Do you want to go in fifty-fifty with me and the kids?" Now I hadn't said a single word to my brother about this and my wife—the only other person in on it—hadn't either. I didn't answer at first, though I probably hummed a bit of music from *The Twilight Zone.* Then I said yes, I'd love to share a canoe.

You might be amazed at how often that happens. There's just something about deciding what you want and writing it down.

I don't know what the future holds. But I can almost guarantee you that whatever happens will be connected to a written goal. Try it and see.

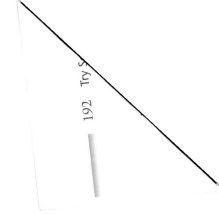

Alesia Benedict

GET INTERVIEWS

Ask some elementary school students what they want to be when they grow up. I bet not one of them will say, "I want to help people write resumes that get interviews." That's what I do, and while it happens to be my dream job, it's something you more or less fall into. I think my training as a director for a big employment firm helped prepare me. But if I had to describe the path I took to a dream job it would be, "I just put one foot in front of the other and when I found work I was passionate about, I stopped looking."

My company's called GetInterviews.com. I'll help you write a resume that gets results, guaranteed. If you don't get interviews we rewrite for free.

So why do I love it so much? I think because it combines everything I enjoy doing. I like taking people who are in an uncomfortable position—maybe they were fired, maybe they're changing careers and it's more stressful than they planned, maybe they're just out of school and have no idea ᴨat job to go after and how—and making them comfortable. There's nothing more rewarding than having a client who's been struggling call me and say, "I sent out three resumes and I have an interview on Tuesday."

The relationship I have with my clients is unique. It's very intense for a short period of time. It isn't a long-term friendship, but it is a life-changing connection. During a critical time we have a tight bond. Most of my clients say, "I love working with you, Alesia. It's been great. I hope I never see you again."

The thing I love most about the actual work is this: My clients, who are now getting interviews, are the same people they were before they came to me for help. They haven't changed. Their skills are the same, their experience is the same, their education and credentials—the same. The only thing that's different is how they see themselves—as resources for employers—and how they package themselves as a result of that new perspective. They see themselves, as Dick Bolles would say, as people with gifts.

I think my gift is helping them realize it. That's satisfaction, to have someone look over the resume or cover letter we've crafted from this new vantage point and exclaim, "I never realized how much I have to offer! I would hire me!" When you can take one of the most stressful times in a person's life and make it an experience for which they're thankful, it's a great feeling.

Most people use what I call the prayer method to find a job. They send out a resume and pray they get an interview. I can help them with a plan and show them how to follow up on that plan, but if they won't get on the phone or get out there and meet with people they're kidding themselves. It may seem easier to sit back and say, "If it's meant to be it'll happen." Most people don't enlist the help of someone like me until that approach hasn't worked. It's because things aren't happening that they show up at my office, and I don't generally have trouble motivating clients to do the hard work necessary to find a job.

One of the hardest parts of that work is putting aside the humility many of us were brought up to think is a virtue. Or we just haven't thought about our accomplishments at all. Take your day. This one. You probably went into the office, got your coffee, sat down, and did your job. Then you went home and did the rest of your life. But you didn't stop and ask yourself, "What did I do today that was noteworthy?" You might think it was silly and say everyone else works hard too—so what's the big deal? But when you lose your job you're going to have to reach back and remember those things. You'll have to come up with a list of accomplishments. Know this. It will be easier to keep track of them as you go along. The stress of getting laid off isn't going to help your memory.

Give yourself a gift on the first day of any new job. Start a daily or weekly log of what you're contributing. It could just be a few phrases jotted on your calendar. Think of it as employment insurance. It won't hurt to have your accomplishments top of mind when it's time for your salary review, either.

You always have to look at yourself and your background and your accomplishments through the eyes of a potential employer. The biggest mistake people who come to me for advice make is that when they package themselves, they focus on the wrong things. They drone on in an interview, for example, about how they got involved in this project or that one—and how many hours they worked. An employer doesn't care about that. Employers care about the results. Did this person get results? Can he or she do the same for me, in this position, at my company?

My job is to help job candidates see themselves in terms of what they have accomplished. That not only helps them get employers interested in them, but it helps them have confidence when they're in front of those employers. It's a matter of remembering what you've done and then putting it in the best light. We take ourselves for granted, I think. And it's not like an employer's going to say, "Oh, by the way, what about that box of awards you have in your basement that you forgot to tell me about? Why haven't you mentioned raising 200 percent of your goal when you directed this year's United Way campaign?"

I'm a career coach in the truest sense of the word. I'll show you your magnificence—and cheer you on from the sidelines on your way to your dream job.

Shane Eversfield

ZENDURANCE

I majored in confusion at the University of Maryland for three semesters. I worked at UPS at night to put myself through school and was making more money than a bachelor's degree was going to get me anyway. So why was I in college? After some contemplation, I decided my purpose was to learn how to learn. Since I learned best through creative thinking and movement, not by reading books, I pursued a degree in modern dance. From an early age, I've felt that the mind and body are connected in ways beyond even our most advanced scientific understanding.

My mother used to tell me I started out as an old man. If you look at pictures of me as a boy, I do look like a little old man. I'm living in reverse. I'm getting younger with age.

After I got my degree I stayed at the university as an artist-in-residence. I danced with two companies, worked as a sculptor—and kept my job at UPS to support the lifestyle. Eventually I burned out.

I moved to Boston and helped some friends build a re-
cording studio. Then I returned to college and earned a
two-year degree in forestry. Seeking adventure, I moved
to the Pacific Northwest to fight fires for the U.S. Forest
Service on a helicopter crew. Our season went from May
through October, which left winters open for other pur-
suits. I spent them cross-country skiing in the Adiron-
dack Mountains and working for Paul Smith's College—
helping with forestry conferences. A friend had a tree
nursery and I was involved with that for many years during the spring seasons. After I met my wife, who was
from Brazil, we lived on the Big Island of Hawaii for four-
teen years.

I was a coffee farmer in Hawaii. That seems like a bit of a
stretch, but actually it was a great place to blend my love
of sculpture with my forestry background since so much
of the work is pruning trees. I also played bass guitar in a
reggae band.

I've always been an avid runner, and when we lived in
Hawaii I was very aware of the Ironman World Champi-
onship Triathlon. The racing event was held just fifteen
miles from where we lived. For the first eight years we
were there, I wouldn't even watch the race. I knew the
minute I got anywhere near it that it would lay claim to
me. After the last reggae band I was in dissolved, I started
running more seriously. I ran a couple of marathons and
got acquainted with the triathlon community there in
Kona. In 1998 I volunteered on the Ironman course at one
of the aid stations. I came back to the finish line and an-

nounced to my wife that I was going to do the race the following year.

I followed through on that promise. My first Ironman was in 1999, and I was forty-two. I overtrained and got very sick. I thought I was going to die. I'm serious. I cut back on my training enough to recover, but not so much that I couldn't finish the race. The day after my first Ironman, I sat down on our porch overlooking the Pacific Ocean and resolved to address the discrepancy between the ordinary human being and the athlete-artist. That resolve led to my first book, *Zendurance.*

People ask me, "Do you still dance?" And I say, "Yes, I do. My dance is the triathlon." It's just a different stage. I love the creative process of training and the performance of racing. People don't necessarily think of training as creative, but it's more satisfying and rewarding that way. It's also a direct path to mindfulness.

Now I'm working in a bike shop in Lake Placid, New York. I went from one Ironman town to another. I'm not a salesman, yet my job is working on the sales floor. I educate people and attend to their questions, and then they know what to buy. That's very enjoyable. I also write for three triathlon magazines, and still race in many triathlons. The distances range from sprints to double irons—4.8 miles of swimming, 224 miles of biking, and a 52.4-mile run.

I am certified as a bike fit technician, and I enjoy that work very much. Bike fitting, like dance, takes place in a studio—and the focus is on movement. The dance is between a human and a bike. I love it so much I've launched Zendurance Cycling, which offers clinics and instructional DVDs to help triathletes with cycling technique. I help athletes cultivate mindfulness to improve their technique, regardless of the sport, which leads to better performance *with less effort.*

The progression from modern dance to triathlon has brought me full circle: Movement is a powerful way of conditioning the mind. I discovered this through my practice of tai chi, which I've been doing for thirty years. It's the best investment I ever made. I don't have much in the way of material possessions. I don't own a house. I have a van that's almost twenty years old. But I do have tremendous health and balance in my life, and I attribute that to the study of tai chi and the lifelong choice to follow my dreams.

Meditation is increasingly suggested as a way to good health, and I agree that it is. But ask anybody to simply sit quietly and focus on his or her breathing. Most of us last about five seconds. It's just too difficult to quiet that little voice inside your head, with its nonstop, incessant commentary on everything. I think mindful movement works much better. We find a place of inner stillness by discovering our grace through movement.

People often ask me why I do ultradistance triathlons, and I tell them I love exploring the wilderness of endurance and mindfulness. I have a lot of respect for athletes in the extreme sports. If their minds slip up and they panic, it's over. As long as they can remain relaxed and present they're okay.

The real game is to be able to take that serenity from the extreme situation, the adrenaline-filled peak experience, back to the most ordinary situations. It's very simple, but also incredibly difficult. You have to stay present. Remember to befriend the fear and the uncertainty rather than fighting them. Without some stress, fear, and uncertainty, there is no growth.

I encourage people to get out there and get in the game, whatever your game may be. Have fun, and learn a lot. Make *that* your lifelong career.

Kenn Amdahl

REJECTION COLLECTION

I was in commercial real estate, and then I wasn't. I had a rather spectacular failure and needed to do something else. Writing a book was on my list of things to do before I die, so I wrote one. It was a science fiction novel, and I enjoyed the heck out of it. It was much more fulfilling than selling a shopping center.

That novel was rejected twenty-eight times. This is probably the part where you expect me to say, "And the twenty-ninth person I showed it to said yes." Except that isn't how this story turned out. After the twenty-eighth rejection I decided these people were right. I put the book in a desk drawer and forgot about it.

I was rejected, but not dejected. Which sounds like an Arlo Guthrie song, but it's the truth. I decided I'd just have to write something different. I took my kids to see *Star Wars* and was struck by how much they learned. What if you could make a textbook as exciting as a *Star Wars* movie? It seemed like something worth doing.

I picked the dullest subject I could think of, electronics, and wrote another book. This time I got eighty-nine rejections. Eighty-nine! The first couple of dozen kind of hurt my feelings, and I thought, "Well, we can't have that." So I made it a game. I started collecting rejections. I knew I didn't have control over people telling me yes, they'd publish my book, but by God they couldn't say no unless I sent it out again—so I did.

I wasn't sure about my science fiction novel. But *There Are No Electrons* was different. I knew it was a good book, and I knew it made learning electronics more fun. So I published it myself.

I had done the math. Something like 50,000 students— at least—are taking their first course in electronics every year, and I believed every one of them could benefit from my book.

The publishers might not have agreed, but community colleges did. Pretty soon the orders came in. It's a pretty easy business, really. You only have to write a book once, after all. I get up in the morning, have a cup of coffee, and go down to the computer or fax machine to see how many orders are waiting.

Some of the eighty-nine publishers have been back in touch. "We've kind of rethought that electronics book," they'll say. They see these good reviews and the sales figures, and what would I think about taking $3,000 in exchange for giving them the right to publish it after all? Where should they send the papers? And I say, "You know

what, I'm making more money than that every month."
Then I tell them, "I hate to reject you, but unfortunately
your company doesn't fit in our plans at this time." I had
one agent call me and say, "Kenn, let me take that book
and sell it to a real publisher. I know I can get you a quarter of a million dollars for it." I did more math and told
her I couldn't afford to sell it for that.

I think a lot of us talk ourselves out of a dream because of
some distant obstacle that may or may not materialize.
"It's hard to make a living as a writer," we think, "so I'm
not even going to write that first paragraph." It would
be like aspiring to run the Boston Marathon, but getting
spooked—because after the race you know you'll want a
good meal and you don't know where the best restaurants
are in Boston. So you don't go out for a jog today. Take it
one step at a time and see if a lot of what you're worried
about doesn't fall away.

Failing at commercial real estate was a gift. I love writing.
It's better than eating ice cream. The best part is having
an excuse to do it. There are people who get paid to watch
football, and I consider myself just as lucky.

I love the freedom, I love not having a boss, I love not
having set hours I have to work. I love pretty much everything about it. Plus, it makes many small acts of kindness
easy. For example, my book *Algebra Unplugged* is funny.
Not many textbook authors get to stick a wisecrack in
there and make somebody smile while they're tearing
their hair out over an exponential equation. Maybe for
those thirty seconds the parents—who are also tearing

their hair out trying to remember enough of what they learned in school to get the kid through this homework session—crack up too. I like to think it's more than a job, it's a mission: I create family harmony, one margin note at a time.

A Parting Gift

I think some pretty cool gifts are wrapped in pain.

When my first marriage began to unravel, I didn't see that at first. I looked at it as a gift, all right. The kind you open and mutter, "You shouldn't have."

There was no map to show me a way through the pain, and eventually I quit fighting it. I let myself hurt—for seven months. For seven months I had the luxury of doing almost nothing but grieve. Most people told me it was taking too long to move on, except for one—who said it takes as long as it takes. I learned the only way to feel better sometimes is to let yourself feel even worse.

Any four-year-old knows this. Try telling a toddler to stop crying, that it's wrong to be *this* upset about *that* thing. Suddenly you have a different problem.

The opposite is magic. If you tell the four-year-old, "That sucks. That really sucks"—as you scoop the child up in your arms to comfort her for as long as she needs—watch how quickly the sun comes out. As corny as what you're telling her sounds, the bad feelings are washing away and making room for the good ones. Maybe that's why they call it having a *good* cry.

Whatever. It works.

Something hurts. You let it hurt. After a while it stops hurting. Your heart is broken, and there's room for something wonderful to move in.

Which in my case is the life I'd always dreamed of. Work I love, a best friend turned husband who helped me find it, and a daughter who makes it all worthwhile. Everything I cherish is a direct result of having lost everything I thought I cherished. It took me seven months to say good-bye, but I haven't missed my old life for one minute.

That's why I agree with what Louis L'Amour said—and it's what I want to share with you as *we* say good-bye . . . for now: "There will come a time when you believe everything is finished. That will be the beginning."

Acknowledgments

I always feel guilty when I sit down to write. "Shouldn't you be working?" that little voice in my head says. I have to remind myself writing *is* work. It's my work, and I love it so much I'm embarrassed to get paid for it. The thing about writing—or radio, for that matter—is that you're not generally paid so much you can't live with yourself.

The reward is in the work. And in my case, the chance to compare notes with some fascinating, fun people. Thanks to each of you, for keeping me inspired. That your stories overlapped mine, here, is a thrill.

Thanks to Dick Bolles, who taught me everything I'm still learning. To Todd Orjala, who made me glad I changed careers—and helped me find Wendy Lazear. Wendy, you packed so much encouragement into one paragraph that wanting anything else out of life seems greedy.

Thanks to Christi Cardenas, my agent, for keeping the door open, closing the deal, and being a treat to work with. Darrick, too!

To Ellen Kadin, I think *you're* charming. Thanks for making me feel like such a welcome addition to the AMACOM family. And to everyone at AMACOM, for being so good at what you do. Erika, you're a doll.

To Jamie Marks Erickson, my oldest best friend, for wanting in on this project too.

To Chris Shea, my newest best friend, for passing notes back and forth during class.

A dozen long-stemmed roses to Katie Anderson, for the look on your face when you saw the book's title page on my computer and asked to be on the review team. Being your mom makes it official: I have the combo platter at the Dream Job Café.

A big ol' man hug to Darrell Anderson, who saw this book in front of me all along. Thanks for what I wanted most, a good story. You're the reason I can't wait to turn the page.

I'd love to hear if the book touched you, if you love your job and want me to consider your story for another edition, or if you're in the market for a public speaker. You can reach me by e-mail, and that address is maureen @thecareerclinic.com. Thanks!

Index